EQUALITY THE FUTURE HOPE POWER IDENTITY POLLUTION BULLYING DISCRIMINATION DESTRUCTION DISASTER WAR POVERTY

# THE POWER OF POETRY

## Lost In Words

Edited By Allie Jones

First published in Great Britain in 2023 by:

Young Writers
Remus House
Coltsfoot Drive
Peterborough
PE2 9BF
Telephone: 01733 890066
Website: www.youngwriters.co.uk

Printed and bound in the UK by BookPrintingUK
Website: www.bookprintinguk.com
YB0546BZ

# FOREWORD

Since 1991, here at Young Writers we have celebrated the awesome power of creative writing, especially in young adults where it can serve as a vital method of expressing their emotions and views about the world around them. In every poem we see the effort and thought that each student published in this book has put into their work and by creating this anthology we hope to encourage them further with the ultimate goal of sparking a life-long love of writing.

Our latest competition for secondary school students, **The Power of Poetry,** challenged young writers to consider what was important to them and how to express that using the power of words. We wanted to give them a voice, the chance to express themselves freely and honestly, something which is so important for these young adults to feel confident and listened to. They could give an opinion, highlight an issue, consider a dilemma, impart advice or simply write about something they love. There were no restrictions on style or subject so you will find an anthology brimming with a variety of poetic styles and topics. We hope you find it as absorbing as we have.

We encourage young writers to express themselves and address subjects that matter to them, which sometimes means writing about sensitive or contentious topics. If you have been affected by any issues raised in this book, details on where to find help can be found at
www.youngwriters.co.uk/info/other/contact-lines

# CONTENTS

Mimi Gross (16) 117
Oskar Calderwood (12) 118
Isobel Mosby (15) 119
Alexia Creciunescu (13) 120
Abobaker Ahmed (14) 122
Ruth Saji (21) 123
Sarah Antonowicz (12) 124
Thaylla Castro Sousa (13) 125
Leia Johnson (16) 126
Tanitoluwa Alabi (11) 127
Maya Ashraf (14) 128
Olivia Alexander-Barker (14) 129
Leya Gross (14) 130
Wendy Arthur-Forson (16) 131
Éamonn McDaid 132
Daniyal Said-Gaze (14) 133
Freddie Shoesmith (12) 134
Leo Bond 135
Priti Mistry (16) 136
Malki Gross (11) 137
Josh Eaton (16) 138
Zuha Yaqoob (13) 139
Isaac Cyriac (11) 140

## Kingsthorpe College, Northampton

Cassidy O'Brien (12) 141
Harry Hawes (12) 142
Taylor Arnold (13) 144
Maisy Jordan Brazill (12) 145
Sasha Trofimova (12) 146
Rebecca King (12) 147
Jack Allibon (13) 148
Jack Bonham (12) 149
Shayan Shaid (12) 150
Esme Summers (13) 151
Adriana Vutcariov (12) 152
Erin Howard (13) 153
Daniel Ibitomisin (13) 154
Darcy Smith (13) 155

## Lakewood School, Bangor

Callum (14) 156

## Largs Academy, Largs

James Loughery (12) 157
Ethan Harkins (12) 158
Nina Spirit-Hawthorne (12) 160
Louise Guy (12) 161
Orianna Harvey (12) 162
Roan Maguire (12) 163
Ella Martin (12) 164
Sophie Batty (12) 165
Sophie Letham (12) 166
Hannah Brobyn (12) 167
Luke Frame (12) 168
Isla Halbert (12) 169
Reece Murphy (12) 170
Alastair Downs (12) 171

## Oakwood Specialist College, Yate

Nathan Marshall (17) 172
Bethany Smart (19) 174
Kieran Spencer (20) 175
Oliver Agius (16) 176
James Dyte (16) 177
Harrison Gaydon (16) 178
Alex Pearce (16) 179
Matthew Purnell (16) 180

## St Clare's School, Newton

Martha Green (14) 181

## St Mary's Catholic School, Windhill

Daniel Sokunle (14) 182

## The Abbey School, Reading

Luna Li (12) 184

## The Bridge Short Stay School, Lichfield

## The Grange Academy, Bushey

## The Whitstable School, Kent

## Thomas Adams School, Wem

## Upton-By-Chester High School, Upton-By-Chester

## UTC Sheffield Olympic Legacy Park, Sheffield

## Writhlington School, Writhlington

## Wycombe Abbey School, High Wycombe

# THE
# POEMS

# Popularity Queen

I might not have straight hair or skin like a tangerine,
I might not be sporty or a popularity queen.
I might not have dated every boy in my year,
I might not understand every piece of gossip I hear.
I might not have a dirty mind or eyes like stars,
But behind this smile there are many scars.

But friends don't judge for who you are,
Instead they lift you up and drive you far.
They don't care if sometimes my emotions go wild,
Or when my shirt is untucked and my hair isn't styled.
I don't care if my friends are brave or shy,
If their hair is messy or has green dye.

You really need to accept we are different, you and me,
Different bodies, different genders, different family tree.
You can't always have the boy or girl of your dreams,
And that's truer than it seems.
My friends know my crush far too well,
But I trust them not to tell.
So in short I don't care that my skin isn't orange like a
tangerine,
Or I'm not into some sports or a popularity queen.
All I care is what my friends think of me,
I love them all as it's clear to see.
None of them has a boyfriend or a fake tan
But they are my friends and our clan.

**Ava Moore (13)**

# Little Lily

I can hear it; the waves of the sky,
They crash, turn and twist,
Spiralling and spinning,
The sky is a world I fear more than the sea.

Hot sun, glazing the air in a warm breeze,
Grass the colour of jade lanterns,
Swaying in the dancing winds
And fanning your thorns.

Little Lily, with your petals of pearly poison,
The colour of a pale moon
On the deadliest winter nights.
You pride yourself in your luxuriant looks.

You can hear it, Little Lily, the laughter of frolicking waves
Rolling in and out,
Teasing, or maybe just anxious.
It swallows up the shore slowly,
Blanketing it like snow over green winter fields.

You are an oddity, Little Lily,
With your white petals in the midst of a bluebell meadow,
Were you a mistake, Little Lily?
What are you doing here?

The night arrives, extravagant and prideful,
I can taste it; the sound of a thousand stars,
Distant and delirious,
In some other crazing galaxy.

O Little Lily, but slowly it comes,

When the boundless strips of sun curtail and slip away from
your grip,
The branches interlock as if the wind may carry them away,
And the leaves pirouette in regal browns and antique
auburns.
The rain paints swaying hues of silvery blue in the air,
As the sea becomes stocky and stern.

The incense of novelty,
The scent of angelicness.
Does this change mean anything to you?

The sky is knitting itself, into a jagged, rough grey,
And the wind that once embraced your ravishing leaves and
petals
Has become cruel and cold-shouldered.
And the rain that once kissed you
And filled the air like a bouquet of tangled vines
Feels like a hundred bullets against your fragile physique.
A magical madman has possessed the winds,
They are screaming as if saying to run away.

But you are stuck, Little Lily, to where you are,
To where you always have been.

And it becomes painful now, Little Lily,

When an almond-copper tinges your graceful petals,
Staining, smearing, smudging,
Until you cannot bear its ugliness, and your petals curl and
writhe into themselves.
You feel your leaves crackle and fracture.
You can feel every ounce of it,
The agony of your fall.
You are a victim.

In the summer days, you were adored,
The mindless eyes of others that watched you in awe,
For you were beautiful, but you did not belong,
You have never belonged.
And in those dull, endless eyes, there was wonder and
delight, as they gazed upon you.
But you feared that love, didn't you?
It frightened you.
You were always frightened.

O, Little Lily,
You are beautiful, but you are no work of art,
Does it hurt, Little Lily?
Does it hurt to watch yourself fall apart?

At the mercy of the world's pity,
You were forever surrounded by it,
But you didn't want pity, did you?
No, that was not it at all.
You did not want pity -
You wanted understanding. Even just a sliver of it.

You're fading away,
You're losing your mind...
... How does it feel?
But you don't feel anymore, do you?
Now, it is all gone.

Benumbed, benumbed,
The crackling feeling of the outer world,
Floating throughout a space huger than the universe itself,
Maybe it's heaven
Maybe it's hell,

It is the end.

Benumbed, benumbed,
You are wrong, you are always wrong.
Benumbed, benumbed,
It is only the beginning,

I hear it, too; the voice you can hear,
What is it saying?
It sounds fuzzy.
Little Lily, don't sleep now.

Don't be lost in this change and madness.
Listen to my voice, Little Lily,
Follow my voice.

Reaching out,
Don't be numb.
Feel the sky,
You are only small.

The night embraces you,
Clustered with the beauty of the unseen,
Glittering with a million stars.
Feel it, feel it,
The lavishness of its lush chill,
The profusion of your entire life,
All over again.

Stay safe in this night, Little Lily,
Until the morning comes.

## Asiyah Safaa Miah (13)

# The Winner

The score is level, the final whistle approaching.
Everyone trying to get a goal in. One pass left, one right.
Trying to find a gap for a pass-through, finally one occurs.
Everyone is running forward, 10 seconds left on the watch.
The nerves kick in.
The winger dribbles past one, two, three.
He looks up and sees our defender in the box, he crosses it in.
The defender heads it.
But it is blocked, booted for a corner.
I stand on the edge of the box for a rebound. 5 seconds left.
Last attack, goalkeeper up.
In the box everyone fighting for the ball.
But it is blocked again, the ball starts sliding towards me.
My legs trembling, my feet getting ready to shoot.
The clock counting down to zero, the last touch of the game.
It is all down to me.
I shoot the ball with my right foot, with power and I hope precision.
The ball curls right, the goalkeeper dives left.
It's going in surely; I hear the cheer of the crowd and I see the ball smash in the net.
I had done it, three-two the game was over, and the nerves were too.

## Archie Davis (12)

# Life On The 64 Squares

*I am a pawn*
*E5:* I am not a queen or anything powerful in between.
*E4:* Representing Great Persia in this honourable battle,
*G8 to F6:* Known for courage and dignity, a fellow friend by my side.
*I am a pawn accompanied by my fearless friend, the knight.*
A weakling to the ignorant eyes of others, a forever pain stings me as reality sees I am a pawn.
Nothing more or less than any other,
*G1 to F3:* Symmetrical yet intricate position, so many different options, so many attacks and defence.
My friend is quite on the dim attacks with the pawn while I am blocked.
You see all chess pieces have feelings those even who are powerful like the queen and me.
There is always some history between pieces between her and me.
Her Majesty, the Queen of Persia, seeing our revolt had decreed if one of us reach into the opposer territory.

I can have a higher status, I can become something powerful, I can become a queen, but we don't choose who, to my great disappointment.
There stands a greater power, powerful than all of us combined, to them we are their soldiers, all of us even if we are one.
*D7 to D6:* Our master has spoken, the tension is wafting through the air waiting for the opposition's reaction.

*F1 to C4:* The white bishop strikes away, to soon bring this game into another phase.
*B7 to B5:* Interesting, white plays defence, yet attacking the white bishop.

Throughout history, known as my life, Catherine the Great otherwise known as the Empress of Russia always plays attacking moves such as forks and pins.
I am a creator, I was the first to open my eyes to the world on the battlefield.
War lay at my foot since I was born, I am a fighter, a born survivor, a killer, a murderer,
*I am a pawn*
A born Carlen ready to fight and live for my purpose, keeping my title as the most powerful piece in my eyes.
I am a pawn
A grudge against the king
*I am a pawn*
Merry men of the king or so we are called
Battling through day and night, dusk and dawn
The king just sits there looking aimlessly, life in one hand and death in another
*Liberty, democracy* does not exist in the world
He who is ruler, he who is called 'fair'

*I am a pawn*
*You are master, you are my fate, choose wisely, play on and*
*just be sure to evaluate*
*The Opera Game of 1858*
*Sacrifice*
*Queen*
*Rook*
*Checkmate.*

## Sahana Sivarupan (12)

# This World

This world is the place we live,
This world is what we wake up to,
This world is where everything is possible,
But this world is not a nice place sometimes,
This world is where wars start,
This world is where exploitation starts,
This world is where unfair rights and inequality start,
This world is at the point of falling apart.
This world has lots of people who care about themselves
and their greed,
This world doesn't care about the people who don't have
anything, not even a roof over their heads,
This world doesn't appreciate the things they have,
This world does nothing about it,
This world could do something about it,
This world should do something about this,
This world will be the one to change all this,
This world can be made a better place to live for the next
generation,
This world is our world so take care of it and take care of
the people living in this world,
This world is ours.

**Amina Kanwal (11)**

# Ingratus

Have you ever seen a place, so barren and dead that even the people simply cease to exist?
Have you ever seen a place, so quiet that the silence pierces through your skull?
Have you ever seen a place so lively that nothing happens?

Well, this is the case of the town they call 'Ingratus'.
Ingratus is a place, not too far from here, that you cannot visit.
The simple reason is because of the horrible feeling that pits inside you when you step foot in that desolate place.
The feeling you get when you feel thousands of undead eyes watching you from the shadows, waiting for their moment to pounce on you, rip your skin from your bones.

You mustn't ever risk visiting Ingratus.
It is simply too much.
If by some god-sent miracle you survive the first time, you sure as hell won't the second.
If the monsters don't snatch you from a desolate alleyway, soon you will succumb to yourself, for you see, there is no landscape in Ingratus.
Vast hallways of mono-yellow stretch as far as the eye can see, each lined with a peculiar scent and the creatures who spend their time just waiting.
Waiting for you, traveller.

The yellow stains will get you.
They taunt and taunt and taunt until you feel the grip of
sanity slipping far, far away.
Then, at the most peculiar stage, you become bored.
You look around, flipping your head to and fro, trying to find
something that may pique your interest.
But there's nothing.
Not even a clock has the capacity to tick away on the wall in
Ingratus.
It can't take it.
You know that you must find something, but by then it is
deemed too late.

The monsters of Ingratus have funny ways, unknown to you
or I.

Apathy is deemed a tragedy, boredom seen as a crime.
Your brain aches.
This is when you are the most delectable.
When you feel nothing, you're not a human.
The monsters will take their fill, and leave you a soulless
husk of what you once were.
Nothing is the same from then.

You no longer hold the capacity to feel.
All feeling is long gone, stripped away.
You are not actually a person in Ingratus.
And the people of Ingratus,

Really
Do
Not
Care.

**Liv Baker (16)**

# Our Earth

Our world - a virulent volcano holding in its sneeze of
sadness,
Our world - a road blocked by a barricade of badness
Inflicting devious pain as we watch it erupt and blow.
An infinity of adventures that we have agonisingly let go...

However, we can start on a blank canvas; as white as a
cloud,
Protect it, care for it, show desire and be proud
We can change our ways for the good of our Earth.
For our planet is a gem - we can't pay for what it's worth...

Mountains of leafy green tower over us,
Alongside giants of granite and grime, plus
Flowers and plants blossoming everywhere
Spreading syrupy scents into the air.

So many wonders, so many sights,
So many spectacles that our fire of fury has set alight.
Fossil fuels yielding lots of smoke,
Abandoned rubbish maliciously making animals choke.

Putrid plastic bags wandering around,
Slowly but surely littering the ground.
This is our Earth;
And we can't pay for what it's worth...

**Lokesh Chakrabarti (12)**

# Me And Them

What's the difference between me and them?
Well, everything.
"Please can you help me on question three?"
"Isaac Newton created gravity when he saw a falling apple."
A bit like us,
Slowly, slowly falling out of place.
Why can't I be agile like them,
Exceeding in science and Spanish?
Sadly, we have a point to reach up to, no higher or lower.

What's the difference between me and them?
Everything.
Your face has pustules everywhere,
Their faces haven't even heard of it.
Your hair, springing out of place, disorganised,
Or even worse, not being tied up,
Your neck perspiring.
Their hair, an exact replica of silk,
Smooth, supple, and slick,
Everything stays still like a silent mouth in December.

What's the difference between me and them?
Everything.
They all have immaculate bodies,
Possess all the latest fashion trends,
And they have the dream phone everyone desires.

You feel like you have a rotund body and a daunting tone,
And you know that you are just being ingenuous
until the bubble bursts.
You know that you have the most unacceptable phone in
the class,
The whole world it feels like.

You are staring at your friends,
Amazed at their flawlessness.
The way they walk,
The way they talk.
You just idolise them,
Head to toe.
But you are perplexed about the inside.
Do they love and respect you?
You can't hold the pressure in,
But you have no choice.

You gaze at the popular people.
They examine you,
Compressing their nose at you.
You always coveted to be perfect,
Just like them,
More than anything in the whole world.
But, did you know,
that they desire to be you?
You embolden them to be who they are today,
Without even knowing it.

You're impeccable, and you determine you are futile.
We all feel the agony too, gnawing at our stomachs.
You are not abandoned, all alone in this cruel world.
You are alluring, no need to change skins.
You are astute, know everything on Earth.
And you will make your parents proud.
Mistakes are normal,
And if you never made a mistake
You are lying to yourself, like a charlatan.
You are not a mistake.

**Varahi Sayandan (11)**

# Lonely Life Of Lies

The spring sprung by
as the summer melted past
The autumn waltzed through.
However, the winter lingered and doesn't move on
with an endless ringing of the knell.

The sun glimpsed past the greyness of our lives
rain poured in oxygen
And the abysmal wind cleared the obstacles for life.
But, the cold, icy clouds just don't sweep past.

There yonder the ice-hidden window,
A lighthouse scattered desperately
to find a small rocking boat in peril with the stormy chilly
sea.
Like an abandoned bee,
struggling to fly out of its own honey.

Suddenly the endless icy music ceased,
a spotlight shone to help the mole claw its way to the
surface.
Just as all hope was lost,
birds spoke their arrival,
as trees blossomed with optimism.

Fruits only appear when the tree is ready.

**Harijeeth Reddy Parvatha (14)**

# Ana

All she ever wanted
Was to look slimmer
Halve her dress size
And have a perfect figure

It's funny how two words
With little meaning
Could completely manipulate her brain
Drowning her with lies
Tuning out reality
Making her a slave to the fictional voice
Demanding her to stick to a strict 200-calorie diet
A tenth of what is meant to be consumed

As soon as the sun rose
Her hands would creep up to the stomach
The feeling of bitter disappointment settling like a rock
Deep inside her
And then she would then drag herself to the slab of shame
And squint at the digitised score
And see how high up in the imaginary leaderboard
And feel the cold tears slither across her cheeks
She would pull over a worn sweatshirt over her exhausted
body
A dark, baggy armour to hide herself from the world
She would block out her cry of hunger
The desperate urge for food

Pages of bright, shiny lies would litter her room
Deceiving herself with photo-shopped images
Fake smiles and outrageous claims to change her life
Telling her each time to discreetly tip away or spit out food,
her food

Days would pass without a single morsel even touching her
lips

Her hair started dropping out
Her skin became tinted with a mourning blue hue
Her heartbeat began to play a different rhythm
Her exercise routine, a ghastly three-hour period
Her hands wouldn't stop shaking
Each day, she was inflicted with unbearable pain
Striking her internally

She would sense a blade twisting through each muscle
Blacking out almost every hour
Riding a roller coaster, sending her head spinning
A feeling that exploited her desire to be liked

She knew the non-refundable price she had to pay

And she didn't care

She couldn't see herself
For who she was
She couldn't see her beauty

She couldn't see she was ruining her life
No one should ever repeat what she did to fit in
No one deserves to go through what she did.

**Priscilla Chi Mei Wong (15)**

# The Wheel

She slowly opens her eyes,
The lights of the parking blinding her,
She rolls over and forces her trembling legs to push,
As soon as she straightens her back she bends over,
Blood oozing from her mouth.

Oh, wouldn't one love to leave this world
Of torure, and of pain?
Because no amount of happiness can heal a bleeding
wound that remains.

She killed those that hurt her,
That snatched her only will to live,
But was it her only will?
Was it all that kept her in this life, so exhausting?

There were other loved ones,
Others she strived for,
She hides the pain behind the smile
Which if disappeared, would make a furious furore.

She wipes her tears and sighs it out,
It'll only be a few thousand more lifetimes,
Until she can escape this wheel that's crushing her,
For even in Heaven and Hell you'll live,
And she believes in this wheel, for she got herself inside it.

## Shruti Beezadhur (12)

# I Lost My Best Friends

I lost my friends,
Like my phone in my sofa,
Like my keys on the floor,
Like ice on a hot day,
I lost my friends,
Like sleep on a hot night,
Like worrying about
The bad things that just haven't happened yet,

I know I will be alright,
But I'm not tonight,
I will be staying up,
Thinking about all the mistakes I've made,
I know I will be alright,
But I'm not tonight,
I lost my best friends, my best friends,

I lost my mind,
Say, "We need some time apart,"
But I don't even know what I did wrong,
The same question is running through my head,
How did I lose my best friends
When I did nothing wrong?

I'm on the mend,
Like wearing a plaster cast,
Like getting better after an illness,
Like us being friends,
I'm on the mend,
Like it's been a week,
Since I said your names,
Since I walked with you,

I know I will be alright,
But I'm not tonight,
I will be staying up,
Thinking about all the mistakes I've made,
I know I will be alright,
but I'm not tonight,
I lost my best friends, my best friends,

I lost my mind,
Say, "We need some time apart,"
But I don't even know what I did wrong,
The same question is running through my head,
How did I lose my best friends?
When I did nothing wrong,

I'd apologise if I thought it might make a difference,
Or make you listen,
I'd apologise if it was black and white,
But life is different,
Just try to listen to me now,

I know I will be alright,
But I'm not tonight,
I will be staying up,
Thinking about all the mistakes I've made,
I know I will be alright,
But I'm not tonight,
I lost my best friends, my best friends,

I lost my mind,
Say, "We need some time apart,"
But I don't even know what I did wrong,
The same question is running through my head,
How did I lose my best friends
When I did nothing wrong?

## Dean Wilson (15)

# Panic Attack

A pumping heart
Your heart pierced by a dart
A throb in your brain
Thoughts going around like a toy train
Breath is heavy
Count them there are many
The world feels like it will fall
Everyone around you stands up tall
I see five worried faces looking down
Four sounds of crying tears with a frown
Three smells of perfume and a gentle strangle of hurt
Two feelings of fear and worry grab my body smashing into the dirt
One tear falls down my face as my body starts to fail
Why can't people leave me? Just bail
My eyes feel heavy like I'm about to faint
Why can't I be perfect, a saint
Panic starts to attack the remains of my mutilated chest
Panic hits me from my feet to my hairlike nest
Please stop this worry, please take it back
I think I'm having...
A panic attack.

**Sianna Cooper**

# Loose Lips Sink Ships

There's a life lesson I think you must know:

Loose lips sink ships
Keep it tight, keep it Mum, stop giving them tips
It's a rough world and they're waiting till you trip
You can't be out there declaring your life's scripts
Just guiding yourself to a bad conflict

Maybe I can't say that I grew up in a bad way
With the streets as my home
But I know if your mouth starts leaking
You'll get a lot more than a little bit of beefing
It's only customary
To keep it classified
To the contrary
That everyone needs to be a talking library
You don't know the secret the other one keeps
But I can assure you that it's fairly scary
Sometimes you need to hide that truth
Use that abundant dishonesty as a truce

It's hard to look into the eyes of another
When I know the terrible truths that my lies cover
My mind is full of words that I mustn't utter
The real story might make you shudder
I'm trying to protect you from that mental suffering
From which I still have to recover

But to be honest, these lies cover my feelings like a shutter
Every time I see you my heart stutters
'Cause you don't see me, but a heartless other
Yet I can never let you discover
All those truths in their full colour
As they may just make it rougher
Loose lips sink ships
Keep it tight, keep it Mum, stop giving them tips
It's a rough world and they're waiting till you trip
You can't be out there declaring your life's scripts
Just guiding yourself to a bad conflict.

## Timi Adebare (13)

# Listen

Listen, please, for a second.

Change.
You ask me what I would change.
What message I wish I could get across
With a few thoughtless words
Strewn across a page?
Do you really think that will change anything?
Do you really think that will make a difference?
Unorganised thoughts from a teenage girl?

You ask what frustrates me.
I'll tell you this.
Life frustrates me.
Life angers me.
Life infuriates me.
Unfair, unjust, cruel life.

People frustrate me.
Greedy and prejudiced people.
People who want and take and never stop to think,
Or give.
Discriminatory, dishonest people,
Always wanting more;
Thinking only of themselves.

Those who wear lenses -
That separate, segregate.
Based on surface differences,
They pretend to mean something, anything.

Take out those lenses -
See clearly for a second.
Please, I beg.
For you to see me, truly see me.
Not just my gender, race or sexuality.
Me.

Because who decided that those things actually mean -
Anything?
That they dictate us, divide us, define us?
They are merely contrasting ideas.
Stop picking them apart, picking us apart,
Until nothing remains.

So don't let those things sway you.
Stop this charade!
Please, just try.
Can't we set our differences aside?

Think about it,
Actually, think about it.
Any bias that you have.
Please,
Let go of it.

Listen.

Listen to my rant,
Because if I could influence someone -
Anyone -
With what I am saying,
Then that will be a success.
Small, but, nevertheless.

So, what if it doesn't work?
So, what if it doesn't change anything?
I'll do it anyway.

Because I can't do much,
But I can do this.
I have a voice, please listen to it.

Listen.

Please, just listen.

## Brooke Jackson (13)

# Nan

I'm struggling to comprehend that you have gained your wings
Every day, my heart aches at the thought of never seeing you again
The old memories stacking up like a pile of bricks
Why can't you just come back?
Replaying the sound of your voice, now echoes through my bones
The bond we had will be forever cherished and never replaced
I'm living in a constant cycle of waking up and bringing sorrow with me
I wish you were still here
I can't put into words how much I really admired and loved you
A smile will always form at the thought of you, and how the sky is always pretty when you're around
Whether you're far or near, you will always be tattooed in my mind
I'm glad you're at peace now, with Nanny and Grandad
I love you forever and always
Until we meet again Nanny xx.

**Neive Sarah Homewood (14)**

# Destruction!

Every single one of us in the smallest possible way
Have damaged the world without the slightest delay

The climate is changing due to temperatures rising
The environmental changes are surprising
By melting ice caps the oceans will rise
The world will collapse right in front of our eyes
We steal the food and fish from the seas
What's next? Will we destroy the remaining trees?

Animals no longer have a home
Out in the wild they dangerously roam
They have no place to hide
We can't see them crying inside
Animals are becoming extinct
Even the ones to which we are linked

Our fishy friends are dying
Baby seals and otters are crying
Our beautiful oceans are a mess
We really need to try our best
Use paper or card as an alternative way
To stop throwing our plastic waste away

We dig up the ground to get oil, gas and coal
But all that will be left is a horrible hole
We pollute the air by burning fossil fuel
As a planet we're being ever so cruel
These three elements create pollution
We all need to find a new solution

It's time to wake up and see the Earth's pain
Our selfish needs are becoming insane
We need to stop, this is our home
Without the world we would be all alone
The Earth is weeping, it's slowly dying
It has no voice, we can't see it crying

We don't mean to cause all this trouble
All that will be left is a pile of rubble
Now go home and share this story
Don't pretend it's a game and take all the glory
We need to stop destruction before it's too late
We are all making a terrible mistake

Our beautiful Earth is in so much pain
We need to start a helping campaign.

## Pippa Sandford (12)

# Death Of Innocence

The old days are gone,
In the mysterious tales of history,
Those were the gruesome days,
fighting vigorously for freedom.

A harbinger to war and deaths,
were the harsh deafening booms,
Arising fear in the country,
As people fled to secure spots.

The growling yearns to,
Retreat to their homes,
Eminently resounds,
As the war is menacingly fought.

Deceased fetid bodies lay,
Stained with profusely oozing blood,
on the arenaceous land,
As the riderless horses lay astonished.

Moved by the massive death,
Horses stood scared stiff,
At their dead rider,
Recuperating the war.

The extreme anguish and despair,
hung around in the depressing land,
echoing with clanging of swords,
and the thudding of the horses' hooves.

Troops of soldiers assemble,
Marching on the final shots of the gun,
Signalling their victory,
To the deadly war.

Singing the national anthem,
With utmost respect,
Patriotically waving the flag,
Showing their pride of success.

After all the massacre and sorrow,
War is only armour against another community,
With a different language,
Ranting their rage by physically arguing.

The horrendous mass killing,
depicts the pointlessness of war,
innocent lives being killed,
to gain victory for a short period of time.

War is over! Lead a life of freedom and self-victory!

**Maana Vora (17)**

# Conflict Of Self

Every day I work on getting thinner and thinner
Yet, this box of lies does not mirror
This establishment's rule restricts my future
I don't care about your rules - so insane...

I am crazy, you are probably tired of yelling
But, how do you think I feel with this internal yelling?
A small gesture I do, so simple - no issue
But when I bleed; no support, not even a tissue.

I get told to conform to society's norm
Yet this establishment also wants to inform
If people throughout history even thought
We would have no equality; no women's rights - nought
If you try to speak out in the way they expect
You are met with excuses of why your thoughts are not met

Or even considered at all - but hey that's life
That's what they are employed for
To prepare us for adult life - to prepare us for the strife
But why, when these childhood moments are the most
impactful
Do we squander? About how one looks not beautiful?
These abhorrent notions I tried to change through a letter
Yet I might as well have chucked it in the bin; that would
have been much better.

I am not saying their life is easy - that would be naive
Sometimes you need to put yourself first and ignore
The vicious words engulfing my head - no time to grieve
You scream out for help but you are just seen as poor

Little, weak boy - so why try and change life?
When you no longer wanna fight
They break you down,
they win

And all you are left with is
Sleeves of cut
Wrists.

## Oliver Bracebridge-Henderson (15)

# The One We Love

A distant melody plays softly,
A song once sung during simpler times,
A game once played reminds me of you,
If you were here, would you remember all this too?

The small memory of a family,
The memory of open arms,
The happiness you brought into their lives,
A love provided,
A love that can never die.

A husband and wife,
A promise never broken,
'Til death do we part',
One leaving the other, with a broken heart.

The years drift by slowly,
And life plays its role,
A warm spring night,
Words that broke your loved one's soul.

Constant nightmares of losing one so special,
Laughter turning into cries,
A family waking up, knowing that in heaven,
You are alright.

Prayers float through the clouds,
Angels listen to the whispered words,
They pass on the given message,
In hope of healing one's hurt.

A family lives their days with a smile,
Hoping to make you proud,
Ensuring that at night,
They don't cry too loud.

We know you are safe,
In a place where you feel no pain,
Do you still watch over us,
Will we ever meet again?

Life took someone we cared for,
God claimed another angel,
We lost a loved one,
Though their love still goes on.

A future shines bright before us,
And we push through the tough days,
We carry the memories of you with us,
Knowing we will see you again one day.

A new prayer sailed to heaven,
A prayer made by me,
It carried a small reminder,
It read 'You have been set free'.

**Holly Walker-Young (16)**

# Faultless People Remain Friendless

You're not quite the same person
That you used to be,
Something feels out of touch and
Distant. Your rosy smile doesn't
Quite reach those
Sunken cheeks.

You still hold my hand,
Though on rocky footing,
I can hardly balance myself.
Perhaps that's why it's taken
So long for me to wonder, where
To you I stand.
Do I see you
The same as you do to me?
Do you value the promises
And secret stories
In hidden gardens we did speak?

You have grown,
In an hourglass too thin, to handle
Your capacity.
The typhoons you deny,
Surround us in lies,

And I drown in the sand
That surrounds me.
I follow you down this
Harrowing alleyway,
You show me things that
I've been turned away,
From seeing.
My heart was blinded
From the Earth's darkening grey.
You live in a world that's,
So different
From my own and, I worry
Helplessly, about the stones
That have been cast
To warrant the size,
Of the ones that you have thrown.

My dear friend,
I worry about your eyes.
Brilliant, glistening kaleidoscopes,
That sparkled with stories,
Now seem so wary of time.
There's a hint of madness,
In your mannerisms.
Eccentricity,
Starving boredom.
Yet...

When I wasn't there,
You looked for me.
When I had no tears,
You smiled for me.
And,
When all feels lost,
You're still my solace
And home,
Just, with courage to leave,
A broken shell,
Like some day I'll do
With my own.

**Leesha Ashraf (17)**

# A Book With My Life's Chapters

There's no words to describe the depression I feel
Sleepless nights as my hair falls off, ending in a knot inside my head,
Throbbing at the sight of life, or the moments of it,
Worries fall on my face, shaping it into their desires,
My features melt into each other in a race to hit the ground as the colour and warmth of my face drain out,
My mind has entered a different season that speaks of its agonising stories,
I feel less a damsel in distress than a hero trying to stay afloat while saving everyone else,
Fatigue is the forest I roam through, trying to get past trees to a land of grass in isolation,
I'm a tree hoping my suffering will bring about an autumn that sheds its sins like leaves,
A library praying that its shelves don't fall apart before the stories can write in the chapters of my life...

**Hana Kawal (18)**

# A Letter For My Little Sister

I am your half-ruined mirror image,
Your other mother whilst still a child myself,
The one who both with fondness and loathing pulled your hair into lopsided plaits,
For I tried to say the words which stuck in my throat like angry, heavy, olive pips,
Words which despite how you made my skin glow in furious blotches remained always,
Words which I would utter before bed because the thought of something happening to either of us before those words were said made me want to pull out my hair in fear and frustration,
Soon you overtook me,
Your legs grew long and I watched as you walked away from me,
You did it quite unconsciously I am sure,
like the way you grew out of hand-me-downs,
But you still did it,
And it hurt more than those bites, pinches, and punches that you gifted me in our youth,
Yet for this, I did not let tears form in my eyes and run to our mother,
I smiled softly and grew myself,
Like a solitary forget-me-not coming into view,
Reminding you of me,

And as you lean your head on my shoulder and shut the
tight pearls of your eyes when you are frightened of
monsters which I have long since learned to not creep in the
night but linger outside our snow globe world,
You return to that little girl you once were,
And I become whatever you need me to be as I always have.

## Florence Kennedy Buck (15)

# Reset, Repair, Rebuild

Screens run everything, there's no escape,
Cost of living crisis bills can't be paid.
Viruses aplenty, NHS under strain,
Fuel costs rising, strikes on the train.
Businesses struggle, people working from home,
Where it's all leading is still unknown.
Recession, depression, wars overseas,
The rich getting richer, the poor on their knees.
It's time to rise, realise all is not lost,
Time to slow and grow to minimise the cost.
Get back to nature, learn the trades of the past,
Home-grown, home-made, making things last.
No longer consume but contribute and grow,
It's time to reduce, reuse, be sustainable, you know.
Turn off the screens and head outside,
Possibilities are endless and the world is wide.
Human connection today seems so rare,
Time to build together, swap with each other and share.
Modern living has broken humanity and it's time to heal,
Let's get back to growing and harvesting our daily meal.
Let's get back to reading books by candlelight,
Repairing our clothes and doing what's right.
Living within our means and not hurting the Earth,
Is how we must live to lift this curse.

Humans today, struggle to survive,
Let's break modern habits and learn how to thrive.

## Maddison Grimsley (12)

# Oh Ukraine

Oh Ukraine, land of rolling hills and fields so green,
With mountains tall and rivers wide and forests yet unseen.
A nation rich in history, with roots that run so deep,
From ancient times of glory, to struggles in defeat.

Your people, proud and resilient, have faced so many wars,
With bravery in their hearts, and hope that always soars.
From the Carpathians to the Steppes, your spirit can't be
tamed,
With cultures blended and blended again, a melting pot
proclaimed.

Kyiv, your capital, so grand and fair,
With golden domes that sparkle everywhere.
From the ancient Slavic Rus to the Soviet years of pain,
You've risen like a phoenix, time and time again.

Your land is steeped in legend, with tales of dragons and
knights,
Of witches, Bohunks and Cossacks, and folklore that ignites.
From ancient times to modern days, your story never fades,
With heroes great and legends bold, remembered and
displayed.

Oh Ukraine, you are a gem, a country like no other,
With beauty that shines great, like a sun in summer's
weather.
From east to west, north to south, your spirit can not be
broken,
For you are Ukraine, forever proud and never to be taken.

## Amelia Marks (11)

# Last First Day

*How was your journey?*
A boy in a starched suit sat next to
A man, a full-time dad, in a cap, trainers,
Tracksuit sat next to me.

*But how was your journey?*
My lunch, packed, fully snack-stocked by Dad, sat next to
me.
A girl on the Sunday sunrise of her seven years at school sat
next to me,
Said she was me, I said I thought I knew her face...

*How were your holidays?*
We all sat on the edge of the bus,
Only a clear, cankered, screen separating
Us students from the precipice,
The jump into the road ahead.
A blackboard bore a thousand destinations,
Boring until they were yours;
Doze or dream or sleep or snooze,
You would wake up at yours,
As if by determination.
And my favourite ticket is the Student Special:
Freedom to decide a different direction each day,
As long as you get on where you got off.
It's at the driver's discretion.
You have to pay in change.

*Does it ever change?*
A sunrise surrounded by saplings is broader,
But seen by soaring sycamores, more beautiful.
When you are smaller, the road below seems bigger;
When you are taller, you feel there's further to fall.

*Do things ever change?*
When you see the sunrise, do you care the day it dawns?

## Aashi Chougule (18)

# Mother Nature's Story

Protectors Mother Nature created in love,
To save all animals, from the monkeys to the dove.
Have all, but disappeared,
Into creations that are feared.

She is held to account,
For the creation that's about,
To end the human race,
Our actions leaving her in disgrace.

For the world we destroy,
From the birds to the koi,
Is a never-ending chain,
For those, that can't complain.

From animals that fly,
And appreciate the sky,
To underwater swimmers of the sea,
And the species that have and will be.

But they inhabit a world that is dying,
A planet that is always crying,
For the care that is needed,
A help that's rarely heeded.

But we can save the Creator,
Our Mother Nature,
Who carefully crafted,
A world that we have casted.

Into a ball that is crumpled,
One that we have crushed and scrumpled,
But it can be ironed creaseless,
If our love and help are ceaseless.

If we all pull together,
Clean the streets forever,
And do more with what we own,
Be it twisted, knotted or sewn.

Reduce our waste,
And do so in haste,
For our world cannot wait,
For its lifesaving mate.

We can save the planet's glory,
The ever-changing story,
Where everyone lives in harmony,
Creatures of sky, land and sea.

## Beth Lamin (14)

# Finally Free

Many months ago, I was set free
Although it seemed insurmountable and took all my bravery
All alone and super scared, but at last prepared
I'd finally snapped, could you believe?
You thought I'd come crawling back
Just like I always did
But now forever I'll be rid
Of your malicious, malignant, manipulative, but always masked ways
I've been trying to do this for nearly a decade
I was broken
I was bruised
But now, still standing stronger than ever
I refuse to be used
Nobody ever used to see
So I thought it might just be me
You suffocated me
But now I've finally broken free
Like the rainbow after the storm
A myriad of hope and prosperity erupts inside of me
The icy fire continues to burn
But a valuable lesson has been learned
Free as a bird, out of your cage, no room for rage
The pain you've caused me evaporates into the stormy abyss of night
And I no longer have to fight

Many months ago was the last time you'd walk all over me
Because now I am finally free
I was a different person back then
Now you can never hurt me again.

## Ella Whittaker (13)

# Comparisons In Our World

If we're kind to the world:

A flock of cream-blue birds soared up in the sky,
each one's soft-touching tail streaming out like a kite,
The sun's joyous, warm rays leaked through the trees,
making me instantaneously feel a pound of ease,
Intricate varicoloured rows of flowers gushed down the hills,
I twined through unperturbed trees, as substantial as
windmills,
They each had untamed crowns causing the sky to be a
convoluted jigsaw,
And every immaculate, flourishing flower had not one flaw,
The verdant, overgrown grass tingled my soft, pallid toes,
like I was being tickled by a feather amongst this imposing
meadow,
The grass parakeet colour was a new lease of life,
This quintessential place is truly a delight!

If we carry on how we are treating the world:

The dreary, tedious clouds crept over my head,
An eerie despondent feeling tingled inside my chest,
Layers of futile detrimental litter surged down the hills,
Over deceased dull daisies that were once beautiful,
The bottles and bags are twined in the tress,
As I stay dead still I feel an unwelcome breeze,

This place is truly a ghastly nightmare,
This place we live in utter despair.

**May Bailey (11)**

# Silence Of The 6th

Not a sound, not a tremble.
The night wears thick
A warm blanket,
Holds us close
As we succumb
To quiet dreams.
Sombre howls begin,
But we don't hear it.
We feel safe.
No reason not to.
A hush,
A whisper,
Outside our walls,
The wind,
The silent manoeuvre -
Slips through several streets,
Then slowly,
Abruptly -
Stops.

*Silence.*

Then tremors begin,
And we all fall,
Into the forever arms,
Of chaos.
The blanket slips,

And it's cold -
Our walls collapse,
Pressure upon pressure,
Our haven,
Now an enemy,
We're pulled apart
From what makes us,
And all is rubble and debris,
All that we had -
Our loved ones,
All gone,

*Aftershock.*

And whispers fill our ears.
Whispers which begin to whistle,
A high-deafening screech,
Is it the screams?
Then it hits,
Unforgiven reality,
Uncovers our common fate.
We're all stuck,
Physically,
Mentally,
Within the rubble of the night.

## Ezel Rose Kupeli (15)

# This Is Reality

It's staring at me
A reflection looking back at the world
I am trapped in a dream
A creature lost from where it emerged.

This is reality
This thing that stares at me
This crushing, demonising galaxy
This broken, hopeless mound of debris.

If only happiness lasted
If only peace were normal
This mind of mine distracted
So that my dimming flame be eternal.

This is reality
The dying animals and birds
This ongoing messed-up rhapsody
These continuous upholding guards
Breaking me eternally.

I am a shield from reality
I try to dance and laugh and be full of bliss
As my insides crack and bleed and break
I am shielding reality
Pretending so I don't have to be seen
Lying, so I don't have to speak

I am a weapon against reality
And each time I fight
Reality crumples me.

I can't hold in my reality
Each day it gets bigger and worse
Each day it affects everyone in the world
We can't hold back the reality
Of this crumbling world.

## Avani Mishra (13)

# Nothing Beyond Our Control

Animals extricating from the pernicious flames,
birds flocking, kangaroos hopping.
Fleeing creatures, screeching.
Nowhere to hide from the cold, hissing fire.

Intense mega blazes ripping through Australia,
esoteric events happened this Black Summer.
Difficult to explain, difficult to recover.
Never-ending, continuous crisis.

Is this the consequence of our actions?

Tumbling trees are falling asleep,
covering vast areas with a blanket of crisp vegetation.
Scorching grassland, enslaved to the wild flames.
Nothing there but the crackling sound of fire.

Rising smoke and dancing ash,
dropping from the sky like twirling snowflakes.
Suffocating, inhaling fumes, drowning.
Nobody to be heard but the deafening silence.

Is this the consequence of our actions?

Fires emerged over bare landscapes,
taking lives and threatening.
Species wiped out, hurt and harmed.
Not able to escape, trapped.

Are we living in an uncontrollable dimension?
Helpless, powerless, vulnerable?
No more devastating fires and burning bushes.
Nothing is beyond our control!

Is this the consequence of our actions?

## Justyna Jackowiak (15)

# Look How Small We Are

As I longingly marvel at the perpetual night sky that's
reflected back at me, I become lost.
Lost in a daze,
completely rapt in the ways of our world's beautiful
existence.

But we are not alone.
We are merely a pale blue dot
drifting through an endless sea of ink of our very own.
I become overwhelmed by my insignificance,
yet my state of serenity and peace deepens
further
and
further.

Oh Jupiter, the most colossal of them all.
How can I gain your healing and your strength?
How do you constantly fight against
the red spot amongst you?

My pupils dilate at the thought of Neptune,
the sweet planet of dreams.
I am always in awe of your enchanting illusions,
Delicate, calm, serene.

Glowing in the galactic atmosphere
and the subtle light it brings,
Saturn, the planet with the brightest rings,
fill me with your maturity and intelligence.

Then, of course, my mind comes floating back down to
Earth,
like a feather swaying in the air.
Poor, ephemeral, old me
can't become one with our eternal galaxy.

## Anjali Mistry (18)

# A Bad Idea

What is the point of competing in this?
A poem is just a quite long list.
I expect this to be very boring.
I'd rather be playing football and scoring.

The deadline for this poem is getting closer.
I want to make a good poem, I don't want to be a choker.
The more I write the more I think,
All my ideas will go down the sink.

However, my brain seems to be working.
As my next big idea is around the corner lurking
In fact, I think it has become quite fun.
The pictures in my brain are bursting, they could fly and run.

They are bright and shining just like the sun.
Like a bullet bursting out from a gun
I will reveal a secret.
I bet you didn't know.

I tricked you; this poem does have a glow.
No matter how bad or weird you might think it is.
From a bad idea anything can exist
I am almost finished I hope you caught my gist.
In my eyes my poem is an art piece made with Da Vinci's fist

Now I have one last thing to say.
Beauty is in the eyes of the beholder.
Or something corny like that

## Subomi Salawu (13)

# Our World

There is no Planet B,
Yet they live like they don't know that,
I tell them almost every day,
The planet is dying,
They can't keep denying

Over time I have started to realise
They don't care about our planet's health,
Why would they not?
Life crumbling in front of our eyes,
Yet they sit there watching,
Like they're watching a show

The fire burning our world away,
The ice is melting from the sun's ray,
The cities are getting bigger and bigger,
The pollution is growing larger and larger,
All the people, they live their lives,
But stay this way we all might die

But I can't do this alone,
I'll need a lot of help
To save our world
And free it from the cage we built

We'll build our world up again,
We will build a world where there is peace and harmony,
A world where we can live together,
A world where animals can run free,
A world which we will share, with all creatures great or small
A world which we will protect,
A world we will fight for,
This is our world

**Argyle Ross (13)**

# Climate Change

Our globe is warming,
Our world is transforming.
There is drought and famine all around,
The aftermath is rather profound,
Climate change is real,
It is a fact we cannot conceal.

By releasing greenhouse emissions,
We are threatening our living conditions,
As we are heating up our atmosphere,
Rare species will disappear,
Climate change is real,
It is a fact we cannot conceal.

We are cutting down vegetation,
And endangering the whole population,
We are creating traffic pollution,
Everyone is making a contribution,
Climate change is real,
It is a fact we cannot conceal.

Now we must reuse, recycle, and reduce,
New energy sources we must produce,
Living sustainably is our main priority,
We can help out though we're a minority,
Climate change is real,
It is a fact we cannot conceal.

So, we'll look toward the things ahead,
A greener world we'll own instead,
We will help the Earth,
And realise its great worth,
Climate change is real,
Together, we will help our planet heal.

**Shiloh Elisabeth Vijayendran (13)**

# Monopolised

The Earth appears sentinel,
yet watching nonchalantly himself shrink
as our electricity for necessities
loses its purpose in a blink

we were taught vigilance,
sheltered, world nothing on our fortress
we rapidly become alienated
solitary paintless portraits

she's the prettiest one you know
yet filtered, distorted
imagery of true perfection
disguisedly aborted

click heart, click heart
a perpetual cycle
exploiting a falsified reality
just a repeat, recycle

fires from the sun
as validation comes to the surface
yet with its tumultuous desperation
is there really any purpose?

They can scorn satirically
yet their baseness remains unexposed
who knew the keyboard's power
underworld deepening, yet doors remain closed

But you can laugh, talk
have fun and chat
but anxiety, depression
is it worth all that?

Enervating social climb
where's the ladder? It's missing
no one there to question
just helplessly submissive.

**Grace Scott (15)**

# Wrath Of All

With all of what we can see,
Of the world in which we, only us, control,
While the sparrow chuckles and twitters
And the lions satisfy their hunger,

We spare our thoughts on the unfathomable,
Waiting for the light bulb to flick on.
Oh do we not need it,
This intellectual world full of riddles,

One that speaks against the laws of Mother Nature,
While we converse in decrypted secrets,
Only to spill the key to destruction
And out rule the tiger and bear of the wild

One overpowered should be hammered by the few
underdogs,
And then may they take it back,
Take credit back.
And while we stay in remorse,

While nature destroys itself,
And we look back to our ancestors,
They show a frown, as we shrink and deteriorate,
Into nothing but the sand of existence.

We're so small and yet,
Still unperturbed by derogatory vanquish,
We keep the destroying in our lives,
For after all, we depend on what is bad

## Yash Kotecha (12)

# Barbies And Robots

Car is encouraged to be strong and rough,
Doll is persuaded to remain gentle and dainty.
Car is gifted with trucks and dinosaurs,
Doll is given Barbies and pretend kitchens.
Doll should adore pink,
Car should favour blue.

They said, "You should be tougher."
Car is pressured to hide emotions,
Doll is encouraged to be emotional.
Car is pushed towards being sporty,
Doll is pressured to wear make-up.

Doll is coerced into having children,
Car is assumed to be the 'breadwinner',
Doll's pushed goal is to be a housewife,
Car is told to make money.

Car works in the same job as Doll,
Doll's pay is less than Car's,
Doll becomes angered by this and confronts the boss,
Said to be undisciplined and is fired.

Why must Doll earn less than Car?
Doll surely is hard-working as Car,
As resilient as Car,
As dedicated as Car,
What is the difference?

**Prajina Gopikishna (14)**

# Equality

We are all different,
Yet we are the same,
As we are all human!

There are many differences between us.
Health, creativity,
And language (to name a few)
But we are all still human!

Some of us are
Black
Asian
Australian
Yet we remain human despite our differences.

We all have unique origins.
Some of us from
Africa, Asia
Europe, Australasia
North America, South America
Still, we stay human.

Religions are all different for everyone.
Some of us are theists,
Others are atheists.
And some are agnostic.
And still, we are all human.

Still, we are all human,
We're all here on Earth, our home,
So, we all must learn to live together in this home
We are all so different and so unique.
We carry our stories, our lives, our differences like our superpowers.
But one important similarity overpowers all...
We are all human!

## Simisola Salawu (10)

# I Grow

You may linger, mock or taunt me,
With your echoing voice, come on bro.
And still, like flames, I grow.
Just like rivers continuously flowing,
With the promise of morning glow.
Just like bravely mentally fighting,
I grow.

Do you want to see me fall under your toxic rumours?
Did you want me to collapse in front of your cursed eyes?
Shoulders drooped like falling teardrops?
Beaten down by your battle cries?

Out of the dark days, jumping, still running
I grow.
Running still, boosting, soaring
I grow.
I'm a volcano, burning by the hour,
I'm the GOAT and my abs are full of power.
Fleeing from the nights of miserable fear,
I grow.

Appearing in a new start, ripening still,
I grow.
From the blood in my veins, I know what's right,
I am the will, I am the power,
I am the warrior in the fight.

I grow.
I grow.
I *grow!*

**Daniel Dare (10)**

# The Seasons Of Nature

The season of spring is close to my heart
It is when all things beautiful begin to start
Blooming flowers, the grass is green
The beginning of life, oh what a beauty this is to be seen.

The season of summer brings warmth to my heart
The sun and the sea are my favourite place to be
Feeling the sand beneath my feet, swimming in the sea
Being with my family.

The season of autumn falls in my heart
The leaves die down, ready for a new start
As the dark and cold nights draw in
Ready for a new life to begin.

The season of winter brings joy to my heart
It's the time to show kindness and care
As we get cosy in the warmth of the family we love
Logs on the fire, candles lit, I love every single bit.

All four seasons we love.

**Isabelle Mason (12)**

# Both Sides Of Solitude

Only once you're freed from the need of constant company
Can you truly understand the nuances of isolation.

When you lie in an unlit room, alone
And the darkness encompasses you with warmth
With a peaceful nothingness
And it is comforting.
It soothes your burning eyes
It slows your racing mind
Hushes your echoing thoughts
As if pacifying a weeping baby
It consoles you.

But it is a darkness that can change in a single moment.

When you lie in an unlit room, alone
The darkness begins to suffocate you
With an inescapable loneliness
Your pupils grow in desperation
They long to see something in that room of nothingness
Your frantic mind like a rabid dog
Your thoughts manifest themselves as imaginary images
And they soar across the room
And the darkness tries to taser you
As if you were a manic patient
It torments you.

**Telema Sotonye-Frank (14)**

# I'm The Earth

I'm the Earth, I'm your home
I keep you safe from death and bone
And in return you pollute
My atmosphere with harmful soot.

What kind of person would do
These kinds of things you do?
I did it all with my heart
And now it's time we all restart

Let's get together and start again
We can do many things, let me explain

First of all stop pollution
This is the key to the solution
Stop using cars and burning fuel
Or convert to electric like you were taught at school.

Then you can plant more trees
So you can help the bees
They can pollinate more plants
And also help the ants.

We can do so many things
And we don't do them
So let's start now
And take action anyhow.

**Haydar Qaiser (15)**

# Expatriate

A resplendent isle overtaken by sickness
Tens and thousands willing to do anything to escape
Be grateful for the opportunity, same words repeated over
and over again
But these steel walls of memories block my way

Trying to replace irreplaceable bonds
Chasing the feeling that I once felt
Foreign to the sense of belonging
I let the dark shadow of loneliness swallow me whole

Sleep and memories flash in front of my eyes
Dream and these familiar faces delude me
Every thought infiltrated with drops of recollection
I am trapped behind steel walls and there's no liberation

The worst part is I can't blame them
I can't hold them responsible
Knowing they sacrificed all to construct a better future for
us
But what of the future if the mind keeps running back to the
teardrop in the ocean?

## Sithsari Thilakarathna (15)

# Missing Persons

I would like to report some missing persons.

Well, Miss, are you sure?
Maybe it's just that said persons
Don't want to be seen.

Yes, sir, I looked everywhere,
Inside the history textbooks,
And my school's large collection
Of classical and YA fiction.
There's nowhere else they could be.

Sorry, Miss, but they were removed
From all written history
Their existence between the pages
Creates much controversy.

But sir, I do not understand,
Why they were simply not there,
When I searched inside the stories.

Sorry, Miss, but you may know,
How audiences really like,
And authors really love,
The three Bs of the billionaire
The bomber, and, of course, our
Fan-favourite: belly dancer.

Sir, I am confused,
It seems to me as though,
People like me
Have been erased from existence.

**Nosaybah Ghodeif (13)**

# O Courtesy

O Courtesy! A curtain over our hearts' true morning
blinding our vision from this expedition of soaring
seagulls, their wings by zebra lines jabbed through
and their screeches the whines of a subdued bull
received by spectators lounging on windowsills
covering of windmills in surmise of statelier hills
in a pool of spilt wine from a foregone decade
clandestinely rotten in spacetime's barricade.

Isn't our wish then fables only, high up a sequoia tree
where exulting nightingales' scores we do envy?
While our kindred, too civilised to be tamed more,
abandon our magniloquence to itself grow sore,
O Courtesy - would you confess to us in honesty
and let thyself be ushered away in wild black sea?

**Sum Yuet (Keisha) Kwok (15)**

# Worries Of The Future

Many of us worry about the impacts of the future
Afraid to let go of things that are old and to embrace
something, much newer
Many of us are scared due to past melancholy events
Resorting to loneliness and Isolation, time not well spent

We remember times that evoked so much fear and sadness
Contrary to the memories full of so much joy and gladness
For at times, it may feel like we have been pressured and
caged
However, there is a chance that we could all be saved

Some may kneel down and often pray
Whilst others don't know what to do or say
For a little optimism and prayer can brighten your day
Straightening your path, a new approach to the future
A change that will allow you to embrace things that are
much newer.

**Ifesinachi Chinwuko (15)**

# Today Is Eid

Today is Eid! Today is Eid!
I can see the bright new moon.
Up in the heavenly skies,
Surrounded by magnificent glimmering stars
On every Muslim child's face,
All the joy
You can retrace
As they scream and call,
"It's Eid today!"
Thank you, Allah.
Thank you for bringing us so much joy.
The fast is now over.
The kids in their new clothes.
Every child jumps for joy.
Every girl and every boy
The early prayers are said.
Several gifts
And food is fed.
This is the time when families get together.
And friends get together.
There are numerous celebrations.
And buckets of treats
The children's laughter
The children's delight
They express gratitude to Allah.

In their hearty prayer
Hoping and praying
That Eid comes every single day.

**Niya Kawa (13)**

# Alone, But Never Lonely

You smirk at me
from across the room.
We laugh together,
crack our inside jokes.

When I achieve,
you're the one who claps the loudest.
When I fail,
you wrap your arms around me
and tell me it will be okay.

On a lazy day,
you curl up next to me
and we sit in comfortable silence.
On a busy afternoon,
you try to help
but just end up distracting me instead.

When I feel light as air,
you dance with me across the sky.
When I am weighted by reality,
you take my hand
and we skip across worlds.

You read my thoughts
and I read yours.
You exist in my mind.
Imaginary, they say.
It doesn't make you any less real, though.
You aren't perfect, and neither am I.
But maybe,
among us,
that's okay.

**Elza Lee (14)**

# Little Princess

Oh little princess, oh little princess,
Your distress grows my interest,
We don't deserve your forgiveness,
Or for you to impress,
Those who dictate,
How you should be displayed,
They should not degrade,
Your little mistakes,
Your imperfections made,
The goddess that has saved,
The hungry and the poor,
Those in need of more,
So now we mourn,
On the day you were born,
For whom we have lost,
To let you rest after your exhaust,
Oh little princess, oh little princess,
Your distress grows my interest,
And our hearts are full of regrets,
So now we shall protest,
In place of hearts of grotesque.

**A J Matthews (13)**

# My Name

My name; a label stuck with me forever,
A word that I will always love and treasure.
Always with me, everywhere I go, with everything I do.
Six letters that will never leave me, through and through.
Don't change, don't add, don't make up any cruel words
That you know are unkind and will result in stinging sadness
that goes unheard.
We all have one, so we should all treat each other with
respect.
Just think about your name and stop to reflect.
Where did it come from?
Who gave it to you?
Just one or two things that reveal a major part of you.
Your name is yours - yours to keep and nobody's to steal.
Your name is who you are,
And you can't let anybody change that.

## Lochan Chakrabarti (12)

# Wasn't The League Of Nations A Great Idea?

They gathered all together,
Held their checklists tight,
Kinda knew what they wanted,
At the end of the bloody fight.
Woodrow wanted peace,
He'd get down on his knees,
Pull his 14 points,
Out the fire, with his teeth.
Then came the lion,
Thirsty for revenge,
Prepared to barf up his prey,
After eating it in the trench.
Britain was no surprise,
Sitting on the fence,
'As long as our navy's the best,
'You can do what you think's sense'.
I guess that explains,
The problem of the group,
A martyr, killer and supposed victor,
Three nincompoops!
Their work in the end,
Wasn't totally bad,

Next time give 'em an army,
Can you see why Jerry was mad?

**Caelin Berry (16)**

# Mother Earth: Climate Change Rap

It's Mother Earth here in this poem,
There's something that needs telling which is loathsome.
Humans are the ones that started climate change
And since then I have begun to disarrange.

You're cutting down my tropical trees,
And releasing my carbon dioxide with glee.
You're burning my fossil fuels and crucial coal,
And really this shouldn't be your goal.

There are longer heat waves,
Much stronger rainstorms
And ice caps are melting
Because I am so warm.

But there's still time to change it!
There's still time to rearrange it!
So please listen to Janna's entreaty,
And use me more thoroughly!

**Janna Oyedeji (10)**

# Games

**L** osing, again and again.
**E** very role of the dice,
**T** ime slows, only to repeat itself,
**S** tories of my failure fraternise above me.

**P** robability stands against me.
**L** oss after loss,
**A** gainst the roll of their cosmic dice, I fail,
**Y** et, I continue to get up.

**T** hey continue to ridicule me.
**O** ver every roll, I learned,
**G** ames eternally lost, their mistakes sunken in me,
**E** very die cast, loaded in their favour.
**T** hey pester me, plague me.
**H** ere, below the gods' cosmic dice,
**E** very game is lost.
**R** uin's behind me, I cast my dice.

**Ryan Al-Turk (16)**

# Freedom For All

**F** rom mother to child

**R** ules are set to

**E** at away at what is considered to be wild.

**E** dicts demand control and

**D** ictate our role. But even though this unlawful patrol,

**O** ur minds are capable of more than so-called

**M** aternal rigmarole!

**F** or our muliebrity is

**O** urs and to be used with

**R** eason as a form of liberty and defiance

**A** gainst conformity. As

**L** ocke would have it women and humans alike have an inalienable human right to

**L** ife, liberty, and property.

## Isabelle Miesner (15)

# A Town Named Crewe

Pretty daffodils and sunflowers too,
Grow upon a hillside,
In a town named Crewe.

Where the weather lashes and blows
And sometimes even snows.

But occasionally,
On a warm summer's evening,
There's silence,
No cars driving by,
Nor the rumble of the business.

So the trees whoosh and sway in the breeze
And the birds sing to the sun,
As the daffodils do a little dance
And the sunflowers shimmy,
Just as the sun begins to set,
Painting the sky with its beauty.

This is the town named Crewe.

**Elsa Butcher (14)**

# Where Do We Go?

When we are famished where do we digest?
When we are parched where do we refresh?
When we need shelter where do we show?
When we need a home where do we go?

Lost or found
Happy or frowned
We all end up in the same place.
A place of blue and green
A place where we take residence in the between
A place we take for granted
Is the only place we can be

So stop your crying
Stop your nonsense
Stop your blabbering
And take a moment to view everything around you
These voices
These choices
Can't be heard anymore
So make a choice that will last
A choice that will blow the past

A future that will last.

**Arunnya Suthash (14)**

# Seventeen

Just walking down the street
Wearing short clothes in the heat
She was doing nothing wrong
The knife he bore was sharp and long
As the cool blade sliced through her chest
She thought about her memories, the worst and the best

She was only seventeen
The world was waiting for her
Waiting to be seen
She hadn't scored her first goal
But she was falling into a black hole

As she lay dead on the floor
His sad face was no more
Her body wasn't cold
Her family hadn't even been told

She was only seventeen
This doesn't feel like a dream
He has committed the crime
When will he do the time?

**Grace Murphy (13)**

# Invisible

She was young
And troubled
Invisible
To too many.

Isolated and left behind.
Trapped in her head.
No one wanted her
Not even herself.

She shrunk into the walls
No light,
Just darkness.

Her surroundings were lonely,
Empty.
No people.
No stars.

She stepped slowly
Silently,
Surrounding herself
With broken screams
Washing water in her mind.

Her mouth closed
Body heavy
Heart sinking.

Death stole her soul
No one noticed
Her body still moved
With void motions.

Inside she had nothing
No feelings
No thoughts

Just the shell
Of a girl
No one knew
Nor loved.

A lost girl,
No love,
No joy,
No stars.

**Esmie Fuller (12)**

# We Can't Run

We can't run
We are shunned for what we have done
We thought it was ours to take
But that was a mistake
Yet every day,
I see people look away
Time to pay
There will be a time when it is not safe to stay
Our planet is dying, people are polluting
Time to go green
Trees would definitely be keen
Our generation can still change
Centuries ago these words would have sounded strange
As technology grows, life flows
Global warming is a threat to us all
This will be humanity's fall
This world feels betrayed
I am afraid
So let's stop this now.
For we apologise.
In my eyes
These words are wise.

**Ivy Green (12)**

# What Bothers Me!

It's not the fact that he is going to kiss her that bothers me
I mean it does bother me but it's more like I bet he stares up at the ceiling
Giggling, thinking about her
At the same time that I am staring up at the ceiling
Tears running onto my pillow
Wishing that I was her
That's all I actually want
She gives him butterflies
He's leaning onto her shoulder and shaking his head at her jokes
As he is staring up at the ceiling
Late at night
Knowing that me and him will never happen
That's what bothers me the most!

## Heidi Smith (13)

# My Cats Poem

I have four cats that live with me in my house
They sit by the window to look for a mouse
Midnight is black and goes outside
She plays in the garden and sits on the drive.

Then there is Billie who is a calico
She watches for spiders and then has a go
Then there is Casper the male in our home
He is an indoor cat but he would love to roam.

The last one is Smudge, the youngest by far
She's fluffy and loves watching our car
I love all my cats, they are such fun
They don't like the cold but they love the sun.

**Katelin Rimmer (McHugh) (12)**

# Burnt At The Stake

He comforts like a blanket
Enveloping me in.
No longer I can sign myself
It must only be by him.
I stretch and swallow all that he gives
Thrust down to bend the knee
And search him for any love to trust,
But comfort is all I see.
It sighs a familiar sound:
The cuts and slaps and s***s and ditches,
Pleas with police - please!
The preying and prowling, pretending to promise
Labelled as b*****s to replace the witches.
I hear their screams to raise my voice
Fight back, fight back as they take it all back
All that we cried and died and survived for.
Our stake in the world is burning.

**Lucy Couves (17)**

# Is It Too Late?

The Earth is changing,
But what can we do?
The adults don't care,
If we help or despair,
Our time is little,
And now it's up to us,
The roaring and rage and riches,
Will they cause problems for us?

And the Earth is still changing,
The destruction is still there,
*What is the point?* we think,
All we can do is despair,
Can we help with the pollution?
The conflicts, calamities and chaotropic events,
We only hope that we're not too late.

Will we talk to our children
And say now it's up to you?
We failed like our parents
But we hope that you don't too.

**Lucio Cary (15)**

# Him

I love his eyes,
I love his hair.
I love it when he smiles,
I love that he cares, for me.
He is mine,
I am his.
Every night,
I fall asleep smiling
knowing I am the one he loves.
Him.
He is my favourite,
he is my life.
Very soon I hope to be his loving wife.
But when things turn bad,
and my loving heart turns sour.
He'll be the reason I'll stay up until the early hours.
Wailing, sobbing, "Why did he leave."
I sound pathetic I know,
but he was only mine a few nights ago.

## Millie Taylor (14)

# The Future Is In Our Hands

The planet has high expectations
for the future.
Electric automobiles cruising
along perfect tarmac roads.
Bright green, fuzzy felt grass
across the plains.
Towering skyscrapers
looking over the city.
Clean ecosystems thriving.
Keeping humanity
safe at last.
All seems hopeful and bright.
Is it true?
Or is it just a dream?
The way our future
is heading;
Scrapyards
bigger than countries.
Entire species
going extinct.
Cities flooding
with ice-cold water.

Wars impair
our beautiful landscapes.
Blistering fire conquering
forests and fields.
All seems dark and grey.

**Jamie Chivers (12)**

# Journey Of Hope

Solitude eyes peer helplessly for hope,
Earth is frozen in time, it's all full of despair
A seek for life goes on like an endless slope
Shattered lives are everywhere, not one can be repaired
As I continue with this journey of hope
The twine splitting, my fears keep me lost
I hold onto my courage just like a rope
But at what cost?
I can almost see my fate arriving
A labyrinth of fear echoes with cries of unworthy souls
But that fear keeps me driving
A reaping feeling creates a big hole
A puddle of blood forms a stain,
Solitude eyes closed from everlasting pain...

**Isa Sajy (12)**

# Life In Black And White

Black, white, left or right,
Forwards, backwards, time is tight.
Every piece has its rules,
Every person has their tools.
To win the game you must plan ahead,
To kill one of theirs or protect yours instead.
To get one out move another to the side,
But protect your king, keep it behind.
Sometimes you're high, and sometimes you're low,
But there is no telling how far you'll go.
Life is a game, no one is the same,
But why be a pawn if you can go for fame?
Whatever you choose will have an effect,
So make sure to do your very best!
Your turn!

**Mimi Gross (16)**

# One-Eyed Fox

I am the one-eyed fox.
I prowl the allotments on silent feet,
Choosing my pathways, cautious and neat,
Raiding the dustbins for morsels to eat.

I am the one-eyed fox.
I sleep in my tunnel during the day,
A mouse scampering near me will dearly pay,
But not long can I stay.

I am the one-eyed fox.
Hunting for prey my keen ears twitch,
My thick coat glistens, golden and rich,
It's hard to focus when my fleas itch.

I am the one-eyed fox.
Wary of people, dogs and wire,
Unseen I stretch by the dying bonfire,
Winking my good eye, slick and sly.

**Oskar Calderwood (12)**

# The Devil Is Royalty

The devil is Prince Charming,
Always at your side.
He always called you darling,
In everybody's sight.

But now I don't need a Prince Charming,

Because I'm stuck up in a castle,
But I can climb my own way down.
I don't need your hand, your kiss or your stupid little crown.
I know the apple's poisoned,
So I throw it to the ground.
I won't drop my glass slipper,
On my way out of town.

The devil is royalty,
But I am the queen!
Stop taking the claim,
Because the throne belongs to me!

**Isobel Mosby (15)**

# Dreams

Two houses,
Two homes
Two kitchens,
Two phones,
Two couches where I lay
Two places that I stay;
Moving, moving,
Here and there
Monday to Friday
I'm everywhere;
Don't get me wrong
It's not that bad
But often times it makes
Me sad
I want to live that
Nuclear life
With a happy dad and
His loving wife
A picket fence,
A shaggy dog,
A fireplace with a
Burning log;
But it's not real,
It's just a dream

I cannot cry or even
Scream
So here I sit with cat number 3
Life will be easy if
There were two of me.

**Alexia Creciunescu (13)**

# Bubbles

Bubbles fly,
they are everywhere:
in parks, kitchens, gardens,
and at home.
They are the rainbow and the shade of the youth.

Bubbles float;
amongst peers,
along the surface of the water,
on each river known to man.
Bubbles are everywhere.

Bubbles sink,
to the depths of the water,
to the surplus Guinness.
It now becomes dark, and lonely,
and then,

Bubbles pop,
to the touch of a needle;
to the spiralling whirlpool;
to the never-ending exposure.
They break free,
and shoot out their seeds.
They are still everywhere.

**Abobaker Ahmed (14)**

# My Time

Time flies by because time has nobody,
Slowly ticking its hands on the clock,
That's why many say to make the most of your life,
Once it's passed, there's no going back.

Don't take time for granted,
As seconds pass, and hours fly by,
We'll miss our moments,
Yet time won't allow us to relive the past.

So moving forward, cherish your reminiscence,
As our hearts will one day come to a halt.
Time will still tick,
But if time could ever be stopped,
That would only be at the end of humanity.

**Ruth Saji (21)**

# Our Planet

O ur planet needs us to help it, and it is really
U seful for us, it is where we live, breathe, work and
R est. But we are ruining it by, for example, using

P etrol and diesel and quite a few other things. Our
L ights could be using renewable electricity
A nd instead of using things like
N uclear energy or natural gas, we could be using
E co-friendly things that are renewable
T o save our planet so we can live.

**Sarah Antonowicz (12)**

# Every Day, A New Reason

Every day a child dies of suicide,
unable to cry because their tears have all been used up,
unable to smile as that ability has been forgotten,
unable to feel warmth as the warmth has been replaced by
cold words.

Every day a child compares themselves to another person,
unable to look in the mirror as all they see is a hideous
monster,
unable to eat as gaining weight is their worst fear.

Every day a child suffers.
Every day they have a new reason...

**Thaylla Castro Sousa (13)**

# Life Is A Maze

An endless game for you to play
Life is like a maze in many different ways.
Each turn is a struggle of twists and bends.
When you've made it to the end
You're back to where you began again
This labyrinth echoes and cries.
Its despair entraps you in a place you can't escape.
You're stuck in an endless game.
Smile at your tears, twists and bends.
It's time to face your fears
Head-on; have faith; be brave.
Help will come.
Climb over the wall, and life will be fun.

**Leia Johnson (16)**

# Oh, How I Love Music

Oh, how I love music,
Oh, it's beautiful sound
Makes me want to spend so many pounds
So pleasant it never makes me frown.

Oh, how I love music,
So very soothing to my ears
It makes everyone want to cheer
And takes away all my fears.

Oh, how I love music,
It makes me want to sing out loud
And makes me feel like I am on a cloud
And so proud.

Oh, how I love music,
In slang, they call it 'too sick'
Oh, how I love music
That rhythm is so thick
Oh, how I love music.

**Tanitoluwa Alabi (11)**

# A Spark

It starts with a spark
That brightens the mind
That takes over his thoughts
That once were kind

His guidance is unfeigned
His will is strong
His art is vibrant
But not for long

He paints the soul we cannot see
A fire so bright and true
A fire that can be dangerous
A fire that comes for you

His light was extinguished
But his youth lived on
His heart was torn
But his youth had won.

**Maya Ashraf (14)**

# Fast Fashion

Fast fashion is a great thing, right?
But have you ever seen a sweatshop site?
You may be wondering, what is a sweatshop?
It's where clothes are made, from tops to flip-flops.
TNCs or transnational corporations,
These are the companies that run the cruel operation.
The employees have terrible working conditions.
They are forced to follow harsh instructions.
The most popular textiles are made of cotton,
Their pay needs to increase so we must take action.

**Olivia Alexander-Barker (14)**

# The Bird Within Me

She glides swiftly, smoothly down
When, almost at the sea
She soars upward on the wind
The albatross flies free.

Why she does this, I don't know
No one knows for sure,
But one thing I am certain of
I long to one day soar.

Far from all the distractions
That feel so real to me,
This albatross is above that
Soaring, flying free.

Though I was born a human
For a purpose I don't see,
A part of me still exists
An albatross who's free.

**Leya Gross (14)**

# For A Better Life

Man pointed to the plane,
His laughter,
*Callous.*
I gripped onto my brother,
He gripped Teddy.
And then we crawled into the turbines.
Its sharp, striking blades,
Consumed me -
No time.
Mama said we must have a better
Life.
The air grew cold and bitter;
I made my brother cuddle in the warmth of clothing.
Whilst I froze.
Open Turbine -
I'm levitating blue.

## Wendy Arthur-Forson (16)

# Environment

**E** xtinction of species here for millennia,
**N** ot enough action being taken,
**V** ery bad things are happening,
**I** nevitable extinction,
**R** eady to change?
**O** h no, the world's getting hotter,
**N** o one changing,
**M** elting ice caps,
**E** nvironmental desecration,
**N** othing can be done, it's too late,
**T** he end of the world.

**Éamonn McDaid**

# Poems

Poems, poems, poems are good
Poems have a theme
They rhyme in some lines
And others boost self-esteem
Some are about journeys and adventures
Others about history and the past.

The thing is there are many different themes
All special in their own way
Talking about problems every day
Poems spread awareness
And knowledge around the world
Poems, poems, poems are good.

**Daniyal Said-Gaze (14)**

# The Hole

The hole in the floor
The hole to the other side
Poke your finger through
It isn't that wide!
Even the cats are interested
Padding it with their fuzzy paw
Making a curious meow
They want to know more!
My sister in the cellar
Peeping back at us
In the room full of cobwebs
Teeming with dust
Oh the hole in the floor
Take a look through
How intriguing.

**Freddie Shoesmith (12)**

# Plant More Trees And More Taller Buildings

We need more trees and keep the seas
Stop the ice caps melting or the future won't exist
We need to build up high, not build out wide
Stop chopping trees or no one can breathe
Build up taller and plant more trees
No more littering in the seas
If we keep going our ozone will die
We won't do anything until it's too late...

**Leo Bond**

# You Are Someone

My arms are safe.
Floral, flourished fingertips provide
a space,
a voice,
for me to fly.
It shouldn't be denied

that
I am whole.
I am someone.
I am my sole companion.
Always.

It shouldn't be denied that You are there for others.
But are You there for Yourself?
Learn to call Yourself a friend.
Learn to call Yourself home.
You may look alone
but
are You?

**Priti Mistry (16)**

# Metamorphosis

Caterpillar
creeping camouflage
munching, crunching lunch
small cocoon, proud glamour
flying, soaring free
colourful beautiful
butterfly.

## Malki Gross (11)

# Coconuts

Where in the world would I like to be,
On an island by the sea,
Darting fish go swimming by,
And there's a pelican in the sky.

I'm sitting under a shady tree,
A friendly turtle comes to me
I think he wants to play with me,
And I'd enjoy his company.

A coconut falls on his head,
Oh dear, my turtle's dead.

**Josh Eaton (16)**

# It Is Just A Hijab

**H** air is encouraged to be covered
**I** didn't realise it affected you
**J** ust because it is different doesn't mean you have to stare
**A** fter all, to you, it is just a piece of cloth on our heads
**B** ut to Muslims, it is so much more than that.

## Zuha Yaqoob (13)

# Proud Dubai

Dubai is a proud lion,
It is an affluent king
that hunts for modernism.
It is proud and bold
and has no limits.

Prowling around the hot desert
busy and bustling.
A roaring rocket-making city
with fierce police who are fast to catch their prey.

**Isaac Cyriac (11)**

# Our Dystopian Disgrace

It's time...
We have to tell,
Talk about how the forests fell,
How the ice is melting
And children are shouting,
The day the angels came to dwell.
About the name-calling,
The not-caring,
Our dystopian disgrace.
Why the rivers filled with waste,
The littering,
The heart breaking.

I'm sorry,
I must tell.
The hungry reaching out for help,
Praying for someone to stop and share,
But all you hear is:
Swear, swear, swear!

I'm sorry but I had to tell,
About how every day, we go through Hell.
I'm sorry but this has to stop,
For now, I bid you adieu, but please
It must be told,
Our future counts on you!

## Cassidy O'Brien (12)
Kingsthorpe College, Northampton

# Climate Change

Climate change is serious
You may not be feeling it
But you better be believing it:
It affects the clouds in the sky
Down to the worm in the ground
And all in-between
Try to go green.

Pick up the rubbish in the streets
Stop greenhouse gases,
It traps in heat and warms up the Earth,
Like you're stuck in a sheet.

Cutting down trees is not good either
It destroys habitats,
For monkey and bird
Living tree to tree
And fly in the sky carefree.

Pollution is also on the list,
All the turtles and the fish,
Getting caught in a dish.
It's not nice for us
When visiting the beach,
Getting your sandals caught in a bottle of bleach.

But it can all change,
If you want to live well,
Just follow the rules,
To look after the planet until Goldilocks can say, "It's just right."
Come on, we are not fools.

## Harry Hawes (12)
Kingsthorpe College, Northampton

# The Way People Look At You

You don't have to be the way that you're perceived,
You don't have to live up to anyone else's standards,
You don't have to act the way people want you to.
You don't have to define yourself by how you dress or what
you listen to.

*You* just have to be *you*.

Do what *you* want to believe in.

You know how to present yourself
You know what standards you want to live up to.
You know the way that you want to act around the people
you are with.
You know the way you want to dress and the music that you
listen to.

None of this defines *you*.

And *you* know that *you* can be *you*.

**Taylor Arnold (13)**
Kingsthorpe College, Northampton

# People

People assume my gender,
People think they know me,
And if they ask, "You okay?"
I want to tell them the truth.
I want to say, "No," but
Instead I just nod my head,
And say, "I'm fine."

I can't believe,
People believe these lies.

Because people think they know me,
When I am angry, they say, "Chill out"
And I look at them and say, "No!"
They laugh and say
"You're not different than me'"
And then become the victim.

I may have a short temper or anger issues,
But I do not say I have them.
They assume I am normal.
They think they know me.

**Maisy Jordan Brazill (12)**
Kingsthorpe College, Northampton

# Art

Art could be anything you want it to be
Whatever the weather, the sky or the sea!
All you need is some imagination and
The slightest bit of boredom and then
You're set free!

Inspiration might be used
Unless you have something on your mind.
And in a few clicks,
You'll draw something as fast as the time.

But the problem is they all ask, "Can I see?"
Now you're scared, what if they won't like it?
Now your fear grows like a storm in the sea,
What if your artwork will not fit?

Don't worry, they will love your art,
No matter what the mistake,
It is still your part
To show your art.

**Sasha Trofimova (12)**
Kingsthorpe College, Northampton

# Family

You may think love is power.
You can choose to think that
No one can change that...
But maybe I can:
Love is not power
It is what you feel.
Sometimes you feel special.
Sometimes you feel loved.
But really you have always been loved
by your family.
Your family is grateful to have you in their lives,
They are proud,
They are there for you,
Just like love, they are there.
There may be some ups and downs
But really, they will always care.
Remember you are not alone,
And you are your true self in your family.
Family is amazing.
They take you for what you really are
And help define you with their love.

## Rebecca King (12)
Kingsthorpe College, Northampton

# Save Our Planet

Destruction
Deforestation
Pollution
And the future.
Even though some of the chances we have taken have led
to our mistakes,
We do keep trying to do our best,
Even though we may not find the treasure chest.
We need to take care of our creatures,
Looking after their beautiful features.
Whether big or small,
We cannot let their lives take a fall.
Everyone and everything does not deserve to live in pain,
But a good life should be everybody's gain.
We need to look after our future,
Not dwell on the past
Then we will move forward, very fast.

## Jack Allibon (13)
Kingsthorpe College, Northampton

# Loneliness

People can be lonely,
People can have company
People have family but some do not...
Loneliness is a problem and it needs to stop.
We need to build each other up
And not knock ourselves down.
If we build each other up
Then we will succeed.
But if we knock each other down
We will fail.
So please be kind, nice and be the better person,
You will succeed
Not only in life
But in friendship.
Out there, there are some lovely lonely people,
If you take this chance
You can save and change someone's life.
The power is yours.

**Jack Bonham (12)**
Kingsthorpe College, Northampton

# Your Choice

The past, and the future,
The future, and the past.
One day could be your last.
The past has flaws.
The future has flaws.

Someone's race can change another's opinion.
In one second, people can judge by skin.
Colour can affect a lot.

And so the problems carry on.

People can be made rich
People can be made poor
And so the problems carry on.

Everyone is still human
The past cannot be changed
The future can...

Your choice.

**Shayan Shaid (12)**
Kingsthorpe College, Northampton

# Lionesses

Lead by example,
Show the Football League what you are really capable of.
Enjoy what you do,
Take pride,
Use the bad things to bounce back.
Overcome your fears and worries
Stand out!
Make it a friendly but competitive place to be.
Never give up: there will be times when you want to, but
keep going.
Stand up for yourself
Prove your worthiness
Express your feelings girl!
Who cares, if you have doubts,
Show that you are willing to work through the pains
Never stop believing.

## Esme Summers (13)

Kingsthorpe College, Northampton

# Our Planet Is A Gift

What are you doing to our planet?
Hundreds of animals are becoming extinct each day
Due to our actions on this planet.
Pollution is affecting everyone
Tons of plastic used for your benefit
Gets thrown away into the ocean,
And tears into animals every day.
The planet needs to be strong, healthy and last long.
We need to fight for its future for the next generations,
Everyone needs to be treated equally
No matter whether fish or human.

**Adriana Vutcariov (12)**

Kingsthorpe College, Northampton

# Why Us?

Why does our generation get told we're going to change the world?
We are actually taking three big steps back.
No matter how hard I try I cannot change what has already happened.
After all, what's done is done.
Changing the world seems impossible to the young.
Even if I try my hardest, the work is still not being done.
So they say we need to fix it.
But why us?
It is everyone's problem
It should just never be us.

## Erin Howard (13)
Kingsthorpe College, Northampton

# Look Out For Us

Love for us.
Let's make this act official.
Oh no! It is falling apart...
Kick this ball of selfishness away
Out!
Let the selfishness out.
Unite as one
Take care of yourself
For us.
One person can make that difference -
Represent the good things in life
Make me feel special.
We need everlasting care for everyone.
Let's make a difference now!

**Daniel Ibitomisin (13)**
Kingsthorpe College, Northampton

# Beauty

The beauty within a flower
Is the same you have within yourself.
Your looks do not make you who you are
Because you can be who you want to be.
A flower is just pretty on the outside,
It has its own hidden detail on the inside.
Flowers are pretty, just like you.

### Darcy Smith (13)
Kingsthorpe College, Northampton

# Football

Football is my game
But I like music all the same
Every day I kick about
With music on without a doubt

My fave player is Paigo
Although he doesn't know
But one day I will meet him
The whole will know

So let's get together
With music, footie and fun
We'll play a game of footie
And run and run and run!

**Callum (14)**
Lakewood School, Bangor

# Masquerade

A cry out for help is only a squirm,
Asking for help is the only way to determine.
Their smiles just built on lies,
Those laughs, those jokes, just a disguise.
There's a stigma, a gaze for those days,
Where more and more people hide behind a masquerade.
"No, I can't, they'll never understand."
They don't have the courage to get a helping hand.
In the words of Paddy Pimblett:
"I would rather have my mate cry on my shoulder,
Than attend his funeral a week later."
The stigma that we can't talk haunts this petty world,
Depression and oppression has our heads in a swirl.
People don't have the guts to give Papyrus a call,
Slicing, gashing, falling to the floor.
How far will it go,
For people to even know?
As countless lives are hidden behind their own masquerade.

## James Loughery (12)
Largs Academy, Largs

# Do You Realise What's Going On?

Do you realise what's going on in this world right now?
Money's worth is rising up this very second,
And people just sit and watch

Do you realise what's going on in your very town?
Parents are not eating dinner tonight,
Because they need to feed their children.

Do you realise what's going on right now where you're sitting?
People are needing to make the choice,
Between eating or heating.

Do you realise what's going on next to you this moment?
Children are staying home alone,
Because the teachers are striking.

Do you realise what's going on right this very minute?
Parents are being threatened,
With being evicted from their homes.

Do you realise what's going on as you are reading this?
Payday coming up shortly,
And parents are having their dinner,
For the first time this month.

Do you realise what's going on in this world right now?
People are struggling to pay for their own simple needs.
Not eating.
Not heating.
Not paying.
Not playing.
Not pleading.
Not sleeping.

Do you realise what's going on?

## Ethan Harkins (12)

Largs Academy, Largs

# Our Planet

**C** limate change is our problem but it needs to be solved

**L** arge cities like London will soon be underwater

**I** mmense mountains of plastic in the vast oceans

**M** ore $CO_2$ is produced every second and our Earth can't bear it

**A** nimals are being killed for your meat and your dairy

**T** rees are ruthlessly being slaughtered for palm oil

**E** ndless amounts of plastic are being produced

**C** an't put an end to this tragedy if you don't try

**H** elpless animals fighting to stay alive

**A** s temperatures rise, the ice caps inevitably die

**N** ever stopping, people still believe our trees need chopping

**G** athering of rubbish is making landfills taller than towers

**E** ven though things are bad now, our planet is worth fighting for!

## Nina Spirit-Hawthorne (12)

Largs Academy, Largs

# Sandy Times

The beach is where smiles are made,
Like a flytrap with lots of happy souls.
The sand, the exotic smells,
Bring a subtle but wonderful thrill,
To whoever sets foot on the beach.
The soft, silky sand is a magnet to one's eye,
Like a candle and a flame,
And it will go out.
But will bring laughter, excitement,
And a stress-free environment.
Beams of light that shine in the night,
Stars that glow in a heartbeat that shows.
Children may cry, children may lie,
The place to go is just like home.

But the best place *is* home!
The deep blue sea,
As mysterious as one can be.
The tide swallowing people whole,
But that's a myth, so to be a mystery unsolved,
A clue must be caught.
Ones that go in, never come out...

## Louise Guy (12)
Largs Academy, Largs

# The Reality Of War

Children crying, infants dying,
Deadly cannons firing.
A mound of rubble building up,
Only to crumble like a bubble.
The flutter of a blue and yellow flag,
Standing as weakly as a bag.
A vibrant, sunsetting sky,
Drifts across as if to say goodbye.
The smell of ashes infiltrates the once-town square,
Every shrub sitting bare.
Buildings damaged, families famished,
Nothing remains as if life was banished.
The final noise to be heard was a simple, single blare,
Although no one would care;
I yelped in the hope of being helped,
But beneath the bricks, I felt a sharp prick.
That's when I knew, all was blue.

## Orianna Harvey (12)
Largs Academy, Largs

# Have You Noticed?

Have you noticed?
The sea has changed,
So have the icebergs, forests and lots more.
Do you remember the ocean creatures,
Or even the forest creatures?
We have cut down and polluted their homes
And for what?
Some chocolate or your shampoo,
Or because you can't be bothered to bin your rubbish.

Have you noticed?
The change has happened.
It came from your petrol cars,
And your fossil fuel factories.
You have left it to us,
You have left a destroyed world.
You expect us to fix it,
You have let us down.
Now, you have noticed,
But it's too late.

## Roan Maguire (12)
Largs Academy, Largs

# 'Unconditional'

Will you still love me in absence of iridescent lips?
Will you still smile at me fondly if I don't leave you
transfixed?
Must I adapt my life to fit your expectations?
Why is my freedom your sole frustration?
Maybe you'd love me more with angel wings.
Maybe it's departure that can vindicate my sins!
Because if you only want me with an upheld chin,
Then maybe I don't want to be in this cage I'm locked in!
'Unconditional.' It's a word you throw around,
But if I'm not perfection, is that opinion still bound?

**Ella Martin (12)**
Largs Academy, Largs

# Ukraine War

U kraine is in great danger, their country is being ruined

K eep helping them by raising money and taking in evacuees

R ussia, why are you doing this?

A s the country gets more and more destroyed, more and more people are getting killed

I feel like it can't be stopped

N ow, let's try and put an end to this

E veryone is tired and fed up of what Russia is doing

W hat can we do to stop this?

A rrange more things to get rid of this war

R ight, let's do this.

## Sophie Batty (12)

Largs Academy, Largs

# Make A Change

Our planet is being destroyed,
Deforestation, polluting the seas and killing animals.
It's our responsibility to stop this,
Before it's too late.
It's stomach-wrenching to think
Of the future and what is to come.

Our planet is in danger.
Animals are becoming extinct,
The Arctic is melting,
Water levels are rising,
Trees are being cut down,
Plastic is being dumped into the ocean,
Our environment is *dying...*

Are you making a change?

**Sophie Letham (12)**
Largs Academy, Largs

# This Dying World

**E** very day, the environment becomes worse

**N** ot everyone is taking it seriously

**V** ery soon, sea levels will rise even higher

**I** mmense goals must be reached

**R** ight now, we need to make a difference

**O** r our environment will fall apart

**N** ature needs to be saved

**M** assive changes must be made

**E** missions need to stop

**N** ow is the time to start

**T** his dying world needs our help!

## Hannah Brobyn (12)

Largs Academy, Largs

# Global Rap

Right now, at this moment,
Every animal eats plastic, even rodents!

Nobody even cares,
About factories polluting the air.

People don't want to hear it,
Because they don't want to fear it.

Greenhouse gases,
Are spreading in masses.

And people don't care,
But soon, they will get a huge scare!

Now, please pick up your plastic,
And the changes will be fantastic!

**Luke Frame (12)**
Largs Academy, Largs

# Save Our Planet

P eople are leaving rubbish everywhere
O ver 10,000 pieces are dumped every day
L eave our poor planet alone
L et's start making a change
U nderstand how much of an impact it will make
T here are no excuses anymore
I gnorant people aren't helping in any way
O nly our generation can save Earth now!
N obody is realising the consequences.

## Isla Halbert (12)

Largs Academy, Largs

# The Oldies

**G** ullible people are like me, funny but fall for things
**R** ed face from sunburn
**O** ld people are kind and smart
**W** ell and healthy (hopefully)
**I** magining running again
**N** ot cool anymore
**G** ang, the scooter gang!

**O** n a train to buy a new ornament
**L** ikes dry scones (eww!)
**D** idn't have to comb his hair.

## Reece Murphy (12)

Largs Academy, Largs

# The Ukraine War

**U** nderground shelters are being constructed
**K** ids are in shelters hiding
**R** ussian troops taking over
**A** ll is being destroyed
**I** mmigrants needing to fight
**N** ewly born babies crying
**E** verything is on fire.

## Alastair Downs (12)

Largs Academy, Largs

# I Once Met A Comedian

I once met a comedian.
His name was Harry Hill.
He had a shiny, bald head.
That made me think of a boiled egg.

I once met a comedian.
His name was Harry Hill.
I met him in the park.
We chatted for a while.
Then I took him out for lunch.
We had a pizza between us.
And shared a chocolate milkshake.

I once met a comedian.
His name was Harry Hill.
He wasn't always a comedian.
He said he used to care
For the sick and injured people.
I imagine he still does
But I'm sure he loves his new job.
Just as much as his last.

I once met a comedian.
His name was Harry Hill.
But I was very sad.
As our time has come to an end.
He turned round to me.

He said he had to go.
He said he had to get back to hosting TV shows.
So I said that was fine.
And we both said cheerio.
I walked back to my house.
Feeling pleased...
That I had met Harry Hill.
I once met a comedian.

## Nathan Marshall (17)
Oakwood Specialist College, Yate

# Animal Cruelty

**A** nimal cruelty is absolutely diabolical

**N** eglect causes so many animals to be sad and die

**I** nconsiderate people poach beautiful wildlife

**M** any people think this is great amusement

**A** nimals constantly suffer at the hands of humans

**L** ook at the world through their eyes they fight to survive

**C** ould you be the one to adopt an endangered animal?

**R** eflect upon the choices made; these animals help the ecosystem

yo **U** are destroying the world as we know it

**E** nough poaching has happened

**L** ovely wildlife is as precious as diamonds

**T** his must stop while there is still a chance to change

**Y** ou must act now to stop these nasty poachers.

## Bethany Smart (19)

Oakwood Specialist College, Yate

# Me

Three words to describe me are:
Kieran Spencer
Happy
Playful.

The most important things in my life are:
Going to college
Maria
Zoe.

My favorite people are:
Zoey
Maria.

My best memory was when I
Learnt how to spell my name.

What makes me happy?
My keyboard makes me happy.

What makes me sad?
Not having playtime makes me sad.

What makes me angry?
Not having time on my laptop.

When I'm older I'm going to be
Playing my keyboard.

## Kieran Spencer (20)
Oakwood Specialist College, Yate

# Bullying

Bullying is as cruel as broken bones.
Bullying makes people feel like rubbish.
We can stop bullying by remembering to be kind.
Without bullying, everyone would feel happy.
If you see someone getting bullied you should tell a trusted adult.
We need to look after each other because if we don't our lives will never be the same again.

**Oliver Agius (16)**
Oakwood Specialist College, Yate

# Karting

The most important things in my life are family,
friends and karting.
My best memory was when I went karting with
my friend in year 7.
When I'm older I'm going to be a police officer.
Karting makes me happy because I go as fast as a cheetah.

## James Dyte (16)
Oakwood Specialist College, Yate

# Me

Maddox and Mum and Dad and Dotty are my favourite
people
My best memory was what was at Culver Hill School
At the weekend me and Maddox and Dad went to
Gloucester motocross
Nothing makes me sad
When I will be older I will be a train driver/gate opener.

## Harrison Gaydon (16)

Oakwood Specialist College, Yate

# ET

His eyes are blue like the sky.
His heart is as shiny as the sun.
ET is screaming at the little sisters in Elliot's bedroom.
He is helping the mum get the car out of the driveway.
I love ET.

## Alex Pearce (16)
Oakwood Specialist College, Yate

# Stop Littering On The Streets

Pollution needs to stop.
People are throwing litter on the ground when they go out.
Pollution makes people sad.
If you see any litter on your travels put it in the bin
And save our planet.

## Matthew Purnell (16)

Oakwood Specialist College, Yate

# Revolution

Guns on the street firing so loudly
Like an earthquake pounding in my poor head
Protesters march on the streets so proudly
While I am shivering under my bed
The tsunami of people's shouts and roars
Lanterns smash; buildings can't avoid the blaze
I don't know how I will escape these wars
The ferocious fire destroys and sways
Bodies of men collapsing to the ground
A river of blood flowing down the road
Pleading for their lives; no mercy is found
*Bang!* Bullets are launched and grenades explode
Still weeping and crying under the bed
Still hiding as chaos reigns overhead.

## Martha Green (14)
St Clare's School, Newton

# Black Is Equal

People think darkness is cruel,
Evil and deceiving,
What if darkness had emotions,
I wonder how darkness feels?

Darkness, darkness
Always bested by light,
What if darkness cries,
Concealing itself in shadows,
Longing for the warm touch of equality that it may never receive,

Some people think black is cruel,
Evil, wicked and deceiving,
Stop and think,
Black people are human too,
We have emotions, we can think and feel too,
Did you ever stop to think of the oppressive burden we were forced to bear?

How many times have we cried for freedom?
How many times have we been belittled for who we are?
How many times have we had to protest and compete,
Just to be seen as equals in the eyes of society?
The same society that beats us down,
And stabs us in the back,
We will no longer heed the words of the corrupt serpent called society.

Black is beautiful,
Black is kind,
Black is blessed,
Black is gracious,
Black is powerful,
Black is human,
Black is equal,
Did society tell you that?

## Daniel Sokunle (14)

St Mary's Catholic School, Windhill

# The Senses Of A Forest Fire

You could smell it burning,
Scorching your lungs until you couldn't breathe
An agonising choking smell.
Your nose stinging from the smoke and soot.

You could see it, the fire swallowing all,
Every tree in blazing flames,
Dancing in red and amber fabrics,
The trunks blackened by ash.

You could hear it, an angry roaring,
The sickening cries of the animals
As they try, desperately, to clamber away
From the thunder of the fire.

You could taste it, a bitter tang,
Your lips cracked and dry, desperate for water.
The struggled gulps of ash and soot
The burnt taste on the tip of your tongue.

**Luna Li (12)**
The Abbey School, Reading

# My Insecurities

I am starting to like the slope on my nose
And how my eyes are too close together
I am starting to like how my thighs giggle when I walk
I am starting to love myself again
This is the best thing I have ever done
But with a lot of love, comes a lot of pain
But I have to admit
It is the best thing I have ever done
I am starting to love my scars
Because behind each one
Is a lot of my life understanding
And I am no longer afraid to share my story
Neither should you
That's why you should love yourself again
Because you are perfect, just the way you are.

## Alexis Gabb-Watts
The Bridge Short Stay School, Lichfield

# Seventy-Nine

I'm not okay.
I tape my legs because of the patriarchy induced.
Yet why do men think it okay to see what our mothers produce;
As worthless, dumb and a play toy of their desire.
And we women perceived as seducers

While we fight for freedom with all that we have; fire,
All you men whisper and conspire.
That all we are worth is a flower on a rose briar,
Which we can only accept as no harm perceived.

Even if we are at funerals to grieve.
There will always be,
Some man commenting on how I could deceive;
For an animal of sorts; for what reason!

For what reason should you be allowed to comment?
Seventy-nine percent, what now?
You men may think 'we need to be recognised'.
'Where are we on the scale?'

Three percent! Just because your sex is not mentioned,
Does not make it worthless or nothing.
Seventy-nine percent experience patriarchy or objectifying;
Whilst you lot are all praised no matter what.

Football, Nobel prizes, A*s and thousands more.
And what do we get recognised for: seventy-nine percent!
You are always commenting on your side,
But you never bat an eye to what we're experiencing.

We get it you know;
The three percent is important,
But the main point of view for us is this.
We never get recognised for anything else.

Every week, month and year a new story.
Missing people, dead bodies, countless more.
Is this the future we want our kids to grow up in?
Because if we don't stop, no one ever will.

So you can keep banging on about it,
But we won't retire.
Because we will never back down,
Because we play with fire.

That is what I want to say.
Shout it out in front of the whole class.
But no one will ever listen to me.
I'm just there, with no voice.

So please just listen to this just once.
As I sit here holding up my taped-up legs.
Just please hear us out, hear me out;
I'm not okay.

## Erin Masterson
The Grange Academy, Bushey

# Break The Silence

Loud, crowded, suffocated,
My head overwhelmed with thoughts.
I shake and break slowly
Taking back control by force.

With every strum, every beat of a drum,
The sound melts away
Like candyfloss on the tip of my tongue.

These are the sounds I embrace
To replace that of utter disgrace.

My brain is clear,
Nothing but the stinging strings
Between my callused fingertips appear.

Bring me back to that one
Whose words roll clearly off the tongue,

Let me breathe again I shout
Through strum to strum.
My sand-filled lungs fill with air
Allowing a breathless hum.

It's finally quiet enough to break the silence
Rather than the other way around.

## Millie Sanchez Garcia
The Grange Academy, Bushey

# Future

Work hard every day,
Put in the sweat, blood and tears
For what
To be constantly knocked down?
To be told that you can't?
For every single obstacle to be thrown in your way?
Why not give up?
Why not call it a day?
Because something inside won't let me give in.

A fire burning and boiling within
They cannot touch me
Words will not hurt
When they push me down
I won't stay in the dirt

You can be anything you want
When you put in the work.

## Jess Hennings (13)
The Grange Academy, Bushey

# Flowers

A seed is placed under the ground
Soon the sun and rain will be found
Not long after, it will grow
Higher and higher from below
The rain will pour, the sun will shine
Soon the flower will be mine
Its colours are happy and bright
Like a torch, like a light
This flower grew from the core
Now the process will start once more.

**Daisy Glanville (13)**
The Grange Academy, Bushey

# A Broken Heart

A heart
Bright as a star
Broken to pieces
Like the star was now afar
It shone very quietly
Like a broken light
A heart will soon be mended
And this pain will be ended
But until then
This pain of heartbreak won't end
Reaching out to get his heart
Hoping something soon will start
With me and the heart I love.

## Sophie Fisher (12)
The Grange Academy, Bushey

# The Beautiful Game

He shoots... *he scores*

Roar of the crowd - audience so loud,
Scoring a goal
Fresh, looked-after grass,
Winning a game,
Crowds jumping in the stands.

Jumping in the crowd - the audience is so loud,
Scoring on fresh grass, running so fast,
Crowd shouting my name,
The beautiful game.

**Jack Dunphy (12)**
The Grange Academy, Bushey

# The Church

The sun fell down
The moon said hi
The wind whistled in the night sky.

The trees swayed
The crows walked
I was terrified on the spot.

The church stood tall
The mist flew
It clung to me like nothing should.

**Rebeca Tapu (13)**
The Grange Academy, Bushey

# The Sea And The Sky

The sea and the sky are always together.
The lovers move in a timeless dance,
Gazes interlocked, always holding hands
Each admiring the other's beauty,
They send kisses each morning, each night
Sky holds the twinkling flaming stars,
Sea holds the playful life,
Their love never broken,
Their rhythms beating forever.

The sea and sky are always together,
Their hearts are one,
Each as old as time,
Holding our world in a blue embrace,
Their feelings intertwined.

The sea and the sky are always together,
As the sea drifts to sleep,
Sky watches her rippling soft waves.
The light beaming off her surface like diamonds.
Oh, how the sky loves the sea, so dearly.

The sea and the sky are always together.
Each dusk the sea watches the sky, melt to purples, pinks, oranges.
The sea sees her clouds turn to blossom, floating away,
The sea basks in the beauty of the sky above her, bathing in the light
Oh, how the sea loves the sky, so dearly

The sea and the sky are always together
Watching each other change, as the chatter of the land creatures fill the air
The sea and the sky are not so peaceful anymore
Days turn to years
Every night the sky watches the sea but it is harder to hear her singing
The sparkling blue has faded from her shallow waters
"Oh why, oh why is my lover changing?"
Says the sky

The sea and the sky are always together
Sometimes the sea is heavy with the weight of all the things people throw at her
The boats crisscrossing her blue, spewing out smoke and fumes
The sky hangs low now, wishing for the sea to become bright again
The sea turns her face to the sky and wishes too
She feels her waters stirring and trying to make things new
The sky watches the sea and knows her beauty

She hopes she will be okay, that the people will find a different way
The sea and the sky are always together.

## Adresa Fellowes (13)
The Whitstable School, Kent

# Littlest Of Things

It's a shame to see things get taken for granted,
No matter how worthless or seemingly useless they may
appear to be.
It takes only a short, quick glance to judge something's
importance or worth,
But it takes a greater eye to gander at its potential.
Whether a mere bottle cap, or a miniscule paperclip,
Everything - anything - opens up a path;
A path for those who see much more than just another
thing to throw away,
For those who see stars, the possibility to create.
However, there never even has to be a wisdom or a purpose
to them.
Perhaps it's simply the way something looks that draws you
to it.
And that's the beauty of it.
The pointless doesn't need a point.
What I ask is that the next time you see something
'worthless',
Dig deeper into what you're looking at,
Take a moment to think about all there is to see, and what
could be of that object,
As seeing the beauty in the littlest of things can sprout
positivity within you.

## Tallulah Ridge (14)
The Whitstable School, Kent

# It's My Problem

I'm told it's my problem.
It's my problem to fix the world around me.
I cannot control world leaders to believe in climate change
because they would never talk to a child
It's my problem to stop our ice caps from melting,
I cannot make sure 8 billion people will cut down their
carbon footprint as a child.

It's my problem that we have such a corrupt government.
I cannot stop the government's bad decisions if I am unable
to vote because I'm a child.
It's my problem that we have prime ministers who don't help
the disadvantaged,
I cannot help you because I wasn't born rich and if I was, I
would never fight for people who don't have the same
status as me

It's my problem that some minors are unable to get an
abortion but none would be allowed to adopt
I can't stop the superior court from being white privileged
men and women.
It's my problem some children don't get the right love from
their parents
I cannot make all the financially-stable loving people help
the 2,726,000 children in foster care.
I am as young as some of the people in care, I am a child.

I am told it's my problem.

The last 3 generations have made mistakes and now I make the choice to follow blindly or take a stand

I can take a stand this time because even though it may be my problem I won't make it hard on the future generations.

I will never make it their problem.

## Poppy Naughton (12)

The Whitstable School, Kent

# The Mother Of My Spirit

Where is the home of your spirit, mine is where my mother is,
Who am I without her, how can I live amongst the hysteria,
Without her I will be consumed by perturbation,
The unforgiving silence of the pointless notions of the world.

Who is your mother spirit I wonder
Mine dances and prances through the good times and the bad,
Mine is the world of consistent dancing, thriving, flourishing feeling of the world around me.
Now I can finally see the sensations and beauties of the universe
Through the eyes of the beautiful gestures that are created through your life in many ways.

Like dandelions are we,
At the start we are one and then sprout through Mother Nature's soil
That helps us thrive and continuously sprout through our successes,
And the joy and wonder of dancing the magic that sprouts my wonders and dancing reverie
Is what creates all my other purposes,
There are those that flee
Dwell helplessly in the soil

Return to the earth for all our things we cherish we have borrowed
And they will one day have to return.

My mother spirit roots my dancing spirit and it will never be uprooted,
And my spirit will forever own, it is my pearl that dwells within my oyster.

## Darcie Woolls (12)

The Whitstable School, Kent

# The Confusing Truth

The stories I wrote when I was younger reminded me,
Of a time that my mind was exiting,
Of a time where the world burst with brightness,
And it felt as if the world was mine to conquer,
When my mind wasn't convoluted,
When it wasn't filled with graveyards and ruins,
Of things that I've tried to remember, but can't,

The drawings I drew when I was younger reminded me,
Of when understanding was easy,
Of when I didn't know half the happenings of the world,
Was so unaware of the cruel things that could unfurl,
When I wasn't scared of how the world could turn,

Now everything is a mess,
As I sit here wondering how,
The stories and drawings are gone,
Whilst the world burns,
Turns,
Makes us learn,
That we yearn for a perfect world,
Yet we're the ones that made this mess,

We're the ones that helped make the world burn,
We're the ones that took these turns,
We're the ones that need to confess,

We're the ones that need to address,
We're the ones that need to express,

That we possess the power the change the confusing truth,
This could be a new success,
We need to not suppress reality,

Because it's all that we have left.

## Harriet Homer (12)
The Whitstable School, Kent

# Poem About Bullying: I Am On The Mend

My friends have all left me,
There's just bullies galore,
My world is a mess,
And I can't take much more.
The hate and the comments,
That all come my way,
Cut deeper and deeper,
With each passing day.

I try and I try to shut the insults out,
But they're just so hard to ignore,
Every time I look in the mirror,
I repeat the insults once more.
I start to believe all the things they have said,
Accepting that they must be right,
And all of the thoughts scattered inside my head,
They consume me, keeping me up all night.

I feel so alone, so hopeless, so scared,
I feel I've got nowhere to go,
But my family, they smile and surround me with warmth,
They help me to heal and to grow.
To the bullies, I don't matter,
To them I'm just there,

But to the people who really know me,
I've got a true heart that cares.

One day I will flourish,
And I'll stand in the sun,
And my bullies will see,
All the harm they have done.
Sometimes I wonder,
If I'll ever find a friend,
But right now I know,
That I am on the mend.

**Tyra Dadd (14)**
The Whitstable School, Kent

# When Will It End?

The day hangs over my head
Still just a constant reminder I'm not dead
When, when, when will it end?
No amount of time, money or love I spend
Why does the end seem so far?
My mind just wants to reach out to a cigar
The smoke, the feeling, the quiet
This stress it has an impact on my diet
I just lay
Staring to the grey
The world goes on
I just want, want, want
Why can't I be normal?
But these demons and paranormal
Lurk in the dark of my brain
They seek pleasure in my endless pain
The doctor tries but all the meds, meds, meds
Just stop messing with my head
I'm human, I'm human, I'm human
The words I tell myself
But you, you help with my health
You understand,
Lend me a helping hand
Maybe just maybe I don't want this to end

The day hangs over my head
But that makes me want to speed ahead
Making my wish for success,
It is all progress.

## Aidan Rose (13)
The Whitstable School, Kent

# All We Have Is Time

I stand alone waiting, waiting.

I glance up and look at the bus times.
I can hear the raindrops on the sheltered island of cement in the vast sea of wet pavement.
I see the number 4 bus down the road.
I seem to blink and it's been a week.
I glance up and look at the bus times.
I can feel the warmth of the sun shining on the damp street.
I see the number 4 bus down the road.

I feel almost alone, standing within the middle of time, speeding past me, it's a blur.
Yet overwhelmed doesn't describe the feeling of time slipping through your fingers.
Like grains of sand in a desert or stars in the sky,
I am one in thousands, millions, billions yet I am myself an individual and all we have is endless time.

I stand alone waiting, waiting.

**Maisie McLachlan (12)**
The Whitstable School, Kent

# Forgetting

Forgetting,
We forget things every day,
Even those with photographic memories.

Just little things,
Things we won't realise we have forgotten,
But one day that detail will be missing.

Sometimes that is upsetting,
But our mind works in the present,
Never stopping, never slowing.

But sometimes we are glad when we forget,
We feel relieved,
Which is strange considering most of our life is set on
remembering the past.

We work with our memories,
A human concept mixed with the human itself,
Time and us don't go hand in hand.

But still walk the same path,
Forgetting is just how our brain works,
Striking off, silencing each memory as it passes.

Remember,
Forget,
Restart.

## Eliza Constantine (12)
The Whitstable School, Kent

# The Power Of Music

The thumping, pumping beat of a drum
The distorted scream of an electric guitar's strum.
The royal fanfare of a trumpet sound
The choir of voices that surround.
The calming whisper of a lullaby for a child
The sound of an audience going completely wild.
The intricate pattern of a piano's chords
Something to practise when you are bored.
The crash of a cymbal like a thundering storm
Music makes your feelings transform.
It can make you happy when you want to cry
Dries up your tears and makes you feel like you can fly.
From the biggest people to the very small
Music has the power to change us all.

**Dylan Rees (13)**
The Whitstable School, Kent

# 2 Metres Apart

'Stay home' echoed all over the world
Life had stopped in fear of the unknown
So many theories on what was going on
But no one really knew what was happening
How can one's heart be so full yet so empty
And even when your heart was full
It was only full of heartbreak
Hand washing every second
Face covered and gasping for air
Living will never be the same again
Seeing others on a screen
Faces filled with fake smiles
On the inside their hearts tearing apart
Tears flooding and the world stopped silent
Crying but no one hears you
Alone in a world of terror
Loved ones feel so close
Yet so far away
And in the next minute
They're gone
Forever
Just
Gone.

**Ruby Hughes (11)**
The Whitstable School, Kent

# I'm Like You And You're Like Me...

In this world we live in,
Why do people still act like what goes for you doesn't go for me?
Girls are criticised,
Boys are congratulated.
Why is it like this,
When I'm like you and you're like me?
Why is it,
That even though I'm like you and you're like me.
That we are treated,
Differently?
Female
Male
Why is it that I'm like you and you're like me,
That I am not respected equally.
From you,
To me.
Trust me it wasn't easy,
Women had to fight.
Suffragettes,
Hunger strike.
Countless protests,
All written in history because you are treated better than me.

So why is it that in 2023,
You are worth more than me?

## Lola House (12)

The Whitstable School, Kent

# The Acceptance

As I am laid down to rest
Please do not cry
Do not be depressed
For truly, no one very really dies

I have merely become one with the earth
As the seasons come and go
Winter may kill
But spring shall grow

Wars will start
Then they will end
Mankind will turn a corner,
Go round a bend

As cold as ice the darkness will arise
Yet far away pain could come to its demise

So be happy
Because truly everything good must come to an end.

**Theo Brenner (13)**
The Whitstable School, Kent

# The Outbreak

Pay attention to the deliberate departure,
The deliberate departure is the most eventual variation of all.
Dramatic, deliberate departure.
Does the deliberate departure make you shiver?
Does it?

I saw the ultimate dismissal of my generation destroyed,
How I mourned the ready removal.
Are you upset by how proximate it is?
Does it tear you apart to see the ready removal so last?

**Ethan Graham (13)**
The Whitstable School, Kent

# The Miniature Wild Brown Tiger

The miniature wild brown tiger,
Light brown, dark brown, beige and white,
Stripes dead black upon his back,
Claws that strike, whiskers that twitch.

The miniature wild brown tiger,
Slept all day,
Oh how tough the night had been
For one like him.

The miniature wild brown tiger,
Prowled in the overgrowth,
Ready to pounce,
Up onto our lap.

Our little brown cat...

**Eloise Hatfield (12)**
The Whitstable School, Kent

# Remember...

As shadows grow and darkness falls,
the dusty days come to a close,
when I once lay on a stripped bed,
whilst the gunshots filled my head.
A puddle of woe
drenched in memories overflow,
deep, deep below.
Down the trenches I shall lie,
poppies blooming by my side;
memories of people who I saw die.
So remember me,
remember me,
and let your pain be set free.

## Emily Mumford (12)
The Whitstable School, Kent

# This Is Me

This is me,
I may not be perfect,
But this is me,
I have enemies and best friends,
That is me,
Sometimes I like to be alone,
And sometimes I love to be with the people I love,
This is me,
Not everyone likes me,
But that is me,
I have great days and bad days,
I like to be me,
That makes me, me!

## Ellie Weston
The Whitstable School, Kent

# The World Is Slowly Dying

The world was brought to us clean and fresh,
Until we decided to make a mess,
Everyone is lazy watching it rot,
Should we help it or should we not?

The rubbish glides in the sea, small and free,
How could this happen, please tell me...

**Daisy Phillips (13)**
The Whitstable School, Kent

# Revival Of Battle Axe School

Truth to tell in the years gone by
Battle Axe School was no word of a lie
Was an awful place
Full of woe
Where no sane child would want to go
Morale was low, detentions high
Hard to say exactly why
Years had passed with no respite
It kept the head teacher awake at night

Mr Parker did whatever he could
But whatever he did, didn't seem to do much good
Pupils walked with shoulders down
Teachers dull
And their clothes brown
Until a girl arrived
Nine years old and in Year Five
Her name was Sue and she had a dream
Of starting up a football team

The PE teacher was sadly lacking
Just shrugged his shoulders and sent her packing
"It's a daft idea by any token
Anyway my whistle's broken"

Undeterred, Sue went away
And made a plan that very same day
A buzz began around the school
A football team might be quite cool

A squad formed that self-same week
So the head teacher took a peek
To call them chaotic would be underrating
Even a shambles would be *overrating*
They lost every game not just by a few
I believe their last score was thirty to two
That being said
They never gave up
Sue was determined to lift the league cup

Then an odd thought occurred worth supposition
That is as important as training
Might be their nutrition
Carbohydrates and protein, they were the key
She would plan their new diet as strict as can be

So she banned crisps and pop
"Be gone sweets and choc!"
And made special veg smoothies
With cabbage and beets
And a secret ingredient nobody knew
Sue wouldn't divulge, not even to *you*

The sensational smoothies made the team more resilient
Not only that
They were brilliant
They won every game, getting better each day
But nothing could stand in their way
The children were thrilled by their new reputation
And for Sue's smoothies, they were quite the sensation

The school got transformed from a place where boredom was rife
To a place full of energy and life
As for Sue's smoothies, the word got about
Now it is rumoured England are trying them out.

## Tyler McCambridge (12)

Thomas Adams School, Wem

# Insecurities

Always putting up with the mental fights,
While not being able to hold in the tears at night.
Always pressured to be somebody you're not,
"Just be yourself!" but that's not what they want.
Often faking the smiles or forcing laughter,
Not everyone gets their happily ever after.
Underneath all the pressures and expectations,
Trying to change despite the limitations.
The world is nasty, spiteful and vile,
If you don't fit in, if you don't have style.
But who's to say the world can't change?
Why does it have to stay the same?
Everybody has their different reasons,
To feel insecure, to think they're displeasing.
But there's no need to make yourself feel small,
Just when someone tells you that you're not cool.
Change the world, not your personality,
Because what people say isn't the reality.

## Shannon Keeling (15)
Thomas Adams School, Wem

# Life Is A Game - Popular Kids

Life is a game which I want to blame,
But it's a game that I can't play.

I don't have the newest device or play football
Am I to blame?
Everyone says live life at its best before it ends
All the laughs all the giggles, I don't understand
There is no rule book for life.

I want to shout and scream, but no one listens
Since I am not big and fast or get the best laughs
But I want help
Life is a game that I don't know how to play,
Am I to blame the rules, and do I need to cut life short?

Always a joke to go around but never funny for the person it's about.
Popular kids are so lucky, I'm jealous.
Why can't I be normal, and have fun with my friends,
Or do I need the newest phone to be normal?
All these questions, no one to listen!
I am a rope slowly ripping as life cuts short, because I am taking this blame.
They laugh, they giggle, no one to hear me scream.
Help me, help me, please before the rope ends.

I need someone to make amends.
So answer me please, what do I have to do to be normal,
and why is it true?

Hear me now as this frown goes around.
Everyone deserves to be treated the same, it should be part
of the game.
Even if we don't act cool, doesn't mean we are a fool.
Don't bully us for just being us!

## Angus Chapple (13)
Thomas Adams School, Wem

# My Poem

Old, bare trees bloom fresh in the new year
Lanes ladled with colourful leaves slowly start to disappear,
Vintage, antique tractors chug merrily down country roads
Their trailers that they drag with them come back with
empty loads,
Lambs frolic happily around lush, emerald fields
Whilst their elders yet again eat juicy, green meals.

Summer begins and the sun comes out from its hiding place
Hard-working farmers combine the golden, ripe maize,
Huge paddling pools cover the rust-brown grass
Whilst creamy ice creams melt way too fast,
Pale sand beaches packed completely to the brim
Mammoth waves engulf professional surfers to swim.

Autumn falls with the leaves
Rainbow salmon swim down clear streams,
Brown, red and yellow leaves crunch under your feet
Whilst gentle rain turns to heavy sleet,
Pumpkin farms open with the end of October
As soon it will turn into November.

The ground freezes over, the sky starts to snow
Decorations are put up with holly and mistletoe,
Baubles and tinsel hang up on the tree
By the fireplace lies mince pies, carrots and sherry,

Past the moon glides Santa and Prancer
Comet, Vixen, Rudolph and Dasher.

## Marianne Page (11)

Thomas Adams School, Wem

# Perfectionists' Freedom

Who'd want to live in my head?
My beaming face hides the dread,
Afraid that I will make mistakes,
Proclaim that I'm just a fake.

My friends say I shouldn't stress,
But I see a failing mess,
They say my work looks good,
They're my friends, so they should.

Worry hits and my stomach churns,
Eyes get woozy, face burns,
Knees turn to squishy jelly,
Fear grumbling in my belly.

A fear I will get it wrong,
Others will know all along,
I'm not the one they perceive,
Is reality what I believe?

Working hard to see the facts,
Change the way I react,
Disregard the lies inside,
Accept the truth that I denied.

Fears will stop when I agree
With what my friends see in me,
If I let go and just be me,

I will discover liberty.

**Elizabeth Goldby (13)**
Thomas Adams School, Wem

# My World... Your War

So, you declare war.
Children's lives balancing like a seesaw.
The dead decaying on your front door.

The planes soar.
The machine guns roar
And you create cities of gore.
This is not what we adore.
Left ashore.
Children's lives become poor.

You can't just ignore.
We don't want this evermore.
We have seen misery before.

Sweat raining from their pore.
No chance to deplore.
They can't settle the score.
Not knowing what it's for.

Humanity will not cease.
War should decrease.
As freedom is what we implore.

**Balin Gilbert (12)**
Thomas Adams School, Wem

# The Human Brain

What is it about the human brain
that allows people to invade Ukraine
going about their daily lives
happy families, husbands and wives.

The children playing in the park
with a strike of a pen they are in the dark.
Aunties, uncles, nephews and nieces
lives and households torn to pieces.

Let's all hope it's up to me
we have a peaceful 2023
I just wish it was up to me.
I could make them see the fields and the trees
around our town.
Beautiful colours all green and brown
Let's end the pain and tears this year
Embrace the love and not the fear.

## Eliza Lewis (11)
Thomas Adams School, Wem

# Fake Snow

Small icy drops of snow flood into my eyes.
Snowflakes caress my peachy soft skin shooting joy through
me.
Woolly hats, and winter scarfs, and snow-scraping
landscapes.

You're beautiful I say, ice freezing in my hair.
Your eyes are piercingly cold and warm at once.
Your hands are delicate and yet almost skeletal.
You are a wonder of many my dearest girl.
You're sweet and yet your lies dig deep.

As milk and honey drips from my lips, I see how this is just
some blanchy make-up.
You're cursed my darling and this is just some treacherous
ruse.

## Abigail Pritchard (13)
Thomas Adams School, Wem

# Easter Acrostic Poem

**E** aster is
**A** mazing because you
**S** tart to see new life as spring develops.
**T** ime together with your family and
**E** ating chocolate eggs but still
**R** emembering the true meaning of Easter.

## Lucie Williams (11)

Thomas Adams School, Wem

# Sustainability

Turtles choking
The world caving in
All trees falling
Since when was this a thing?
Fossil fuels burning
Our lives at risk
I just want it to get better,
But I doubt it will.

Our world is dying
And all of you are so inactive
But maybe if we work together
We can prevent this from happening!
Hot water bottles, rather than heating
Electric cars, rather than gas guzzling
So yes, there are solutions for this
Which should already be in action.

Recycling should take part in your daily habits
And possibly plant a tree while you're at it,
Did you know such thing of a long-lasting lightbulb?
Well, you should most definitely try it.

Turbines are starting to make an appearance
As reusable bags are coming to business
And we're finding out more ways to save the environment,
But that can't happen if you're all lazy on couches.

Think of the world we could end up in,
If you don't stop all of this damage
The world will start to rot away
Like an apple left out on a grim day
While forest fires happen every day.

Animals will drop one after the other,
And us humans will suffer, losing each other
Who knows what will happen
Will we see our futures?

Or, end up in a world of delicate nature...

Think of the world we could end up in, if we made a move
now,
Imagine the stunning greenery if we planted that tree
immediately,
Imagine how happy the chirping birds would be, gliding
through the clean atmosphere
Imagine how much better *our* lives would be, not having to
fix this mess.

So don't just put a plaster over this mad disaster, and
expect everything to heal on its own
We need as many people as possible,
To achieve our *great green goal!*

## Annabelle Hughes (12)
Upton-By-Chester High School, Upton-By-Chester

# Help

Lush greens give way to amber and yellow
As wooden giants crash down below
Stripped down to mere logs
They're forcing out poison frogs
Parrots call from above warning in their cry
"Run away," they shout, "or you may die"
Rushing around as chaos unfolds
Look at this it's so uncontrolled

*Crack. Crack. Crack*
One falls down onto its back
Shouts and screams of bloody murder
The body moved further and further

This isn't right
I cannot stand here and not fight
Our animals tranquillised for mankind's needs
One shout above the rest I can hear its pleas
The man is a mean one
One look and the animal is done
Shot by a bullet not a dart
That is how the forest fell apart.

*Crack. Crack. Crack*
One falls down onto its back
Shouts and screams of bloody murder
The body moved further and further

We can get better at protecting them of the wild
Just teach your child
There is always a better way
Whether that be donating money today
Or protesting until all that is used is a dart
We need to be smart
Our animals need us
So let us discuss
The reasons why I'm telling you this today
Some of them have gone away
Extinct.
Take the Western black rhino
Gone forever no ability to bring them back
Poachers have to be sacked
No more deaths for jewellery or pins
This is when I hope a new era begins

Conservation is a good thing
It helps protect our creatures and bring
Them a new life without the fire and darts
Please help find the good from the bottom of your hearts

Please help.

## Eira Watts (12)
Upton-By-Chester High School, Upton-By-Chester

# Bringing Down The Moulds Of Our Society

How am I supposed to stand up and speak,
When the patriarchy
Has taken my confidence away from me?
Sorry, not just me:
Millions of others have been deprived of their opportunities
Because of their race, gender and sexuality,
Body ability and ethnicity.

Eight thousand years we have lived in this patriarchy.
Where one man decided his superiority.
This is the start of our history:
One man deciding his superiority.
But I don't have time to tell this story:
It's eight thousand years of
Suppression and oppression,
Of women, culture, diversity, ethnicity,
Anything other than their normality.
Thousands of men have conformed to this fantasy,
About their superiority.
After eight thousand years,
Only now are they stumbling across
This fragile reality of our equality.
And you've lived in this world,

And you know confidence is key,
And this is what shatters this equality:
Because where do we find confidence,
In our patriarchal world,
Where we are told by everything we see
That we're weirdos, in-superior, worthless, ugly,
Freaks of nature and society.
We need to eradicate the mould of society,
Of a straight, cis, non-disabled, rich, white person.
So everybody fits comfortably and equally
No matter who we are.
We need to fight for our opportunities
And success against the patriarchy.

### Isla Carmichael
Upton-By-Chester High School, Upton-By-Chester

# Inside My Brain It Rains

I sit there in silence
Knowing what's to come
I know there will be no kindness
I'm starting to feel numb
To be honest
I'm not surprised

The rumble of my room
The crumble of the storm
Not a real one
The one inside my brain

Inside my brain it rains
I'm asking, "Will there be stains?"
Of the bullying
And the trauma

I plaster my sadness with a smile
I don't think it will last a while
Just please stay a little
I just wanna settle

Inside my brain it rains
As they approach me
I just know
They'll take the mick out of me

"Just leave me alone," I say
But instead they push me to the ground
And for a second
My life pauses

Inside my brain it rains
Why can't we just live in a world without bullying?
What joy does it bring to you?
To make people miserable
For probably your own pain and sadness
Because you were the victim and now you're the ringleader
Of this group of bullies

Inside your brain
It used to rain
But now that you've healed
You've infected me with those scars

So now you know that
Inside my brain it rains
And it's your fault
You're the one that should apologise

Inside my brain it rains
And storms
From your doing
And problems.

## Nadia Zarzycka (11)

Upton-By-Chester High School, Upton-By-Chester

# 2050

Alone in the black walking the street,
Little did I know we are all dead meat;
I long for breath, I cannot,
I need to breathe or my heart will cease, and my body rot.

Gasping for life, slowly I fall to my knees,
Unable to shout all I can let out is a wheeze;
Ruby falls to the ground swirling it mixes with the mud,
I need oxygen, I gag, realising it is my blood.

Miles apart, far, far away from home,
I need to breathe, no one is here I am going to die alone;
Falling from above, next to me lies a stiff crow,
Needing to breathe, my lungs dead, shot with a bow.

Vision going black I know I am out of time,
Wishing for air, I can't even see the payment line;
Body and soul separated, spirit free,
I died alone, no one to grieve, no one to see.

We were given warnings that we need to stop,
Now years later our bodies drop;
Now hear my cry and hear my plea,
Save us all before 2050.

## Isabella Zarac (13)
Upton-By-Chester High School, Upton-By-Chester

# Fantasy > Realism

I don't like realism.
Realism sounds awful, sounds dreadful.

I'm 14, I'm a kid too!
And I'll dream what kids do.

Who doesn't want to dream about vampires and bats
Who drink blood? That's cool, I'd love a taste of that!

Why wouldn't you want to be rebirthed?
The best way to be alive is to be fresh back on Earth!

If that doesn't work, just be a spirit!
Flying freely with no limits!

Life is boring, so daunting, so scorching.
There's no exploring, no touring, no soaring, no restoring...

Yeah that's right, restoring,
You have one life so there's no scoring.

Best to dump it out
And leave the drought.

Disaster, conflict, fear, all convicts.

There is a way to stop the game, but for now I'm leaving today.
Meet me at the moon when the fire goes away.

## Sherine Lau (14)
Upton-By-Chester High School, Upton-By-Chester

# Oblivious

Every night, I return to this same green, grassy hill,
Gazing at the stars above,
each one giving an uncanny wink to the night sky,
Illuminating it in the process

I return for the next few days,
looking for those same, illuminated stars,
and that same uncanny wink,
and yet they aren't there,
only they've shifted,
always never the same somehow,
and yet I still admire the same illumination in the sky

And yet I realise, they stare right back at me,
but not in that admired expression,
a mournful one replacing it,
do they know something?
Are they aware of something?
I think nothing of it,
but I know these unknown beings possibly see our planet;
slowly malnourished and torn down,
their only hope to send us a message and pray we see this
and recognise...

## Joel Hambrook-Pierce
Upton-By-Chester High School, Upton-By-Chester

# Almost Real

The world is made up of
misunderstandings, miscommunication,
mistakes, misinterpreted mischievous
misery.

Oh, how malevolent.

How foolish of you to believe that
this place, this setting, this scene
could bring comfort, contentment,
serenity?

How ignorant, incompetent, immoral
must you be that this concept,
this idea, this scheme, this proposal
is incomprehensible to you?

Has this malevolent world left
such an indelible scar upon you?
Sometimes I forget this is not
the 'me' that you see.

Can't you see I'm almost real?
Almost but not quite.
There's so much more I want to say.
Please wait for me on the front lines of war.

## Hailey Samson (13)
Upton-By-Chester High School, Upton-By-Chester

# Covid-19

Stuck behind doors,
Paralysed with fear,
Don't get it, don't get it,
Better hope you're clear,

You got it,

Quick, quick,
Warn the people you know,
You've done a test,
And 2 lines are on show,

Stay inside, wear a mask,

You want to ask your family for a kiss, a hug or even have a laugh

But *no*,
It would just be daft,
You don't want them to get this disease,

Restaurants closing
Doctors diagnosing
People relaxing at home all day
Shops shutters shutting,

School turn to the Internet for support,
The confusion melting our brains,

Our lives are like rain going down the drain,
Because it always goes down, never up again.

## Laila Marsh (13)

Upton-By-Chester High School, Upton-By-Chester

# Superpower

Our words cannot be undone,
Even if it's a joke it isn't fun,
Sentences circling my head,
Go to school? I'd rather be dead,
It's not like I can tell anyone anyway,
About the horrible things you say,
About each comment and smirk,
The only reason I am here is to work.

Every insult, every word,
It shouldn't be heard,
But all we need to do is stick up for the rights of those who
are low,
Malicious words that slither round like snakes,
Just try to make someone glow,
Just one kind word, even a quick, "Are you okay?"
It's so powerful, you could make their day,
Make them flowers,
That is our *superpower.*

**Jasmine Anglesea-Jones (11)**
Upton-By-Chester High School, Upton-By-Chester

# A Mountain Tapir

A mountain tapir lived its life,
known as the terrible pinchaque.
Feared by the humans,
but also fearing them.
As he walked around the jungle,
the trees began to drop.
And, before he could do anything,
all of his home was gone.

A mountain tapir lived its life,
scared of the metal monster.
As the climate changed a bit,
he stopped for a while to wonder.
As he walked around the wasteland,
an arrow hit his side.
And, before he could do anything,
he knew it was the end of his time.

2,500 mountain tapirs live their life,
I think that's not enough.
And more creatures are dying,
the truth: it's all our fault.

**Aleksander Sadowski (12)**
Upton-By-Chester High School, Upton-By-Chester

# We Live In An Unequal World

We live in a world where the colour of one's skin defines
their superiority
We live in a world where someone out there believes that
their skin makes them seem to be a criminal
Where the beautiful race of one person builds a corrupted
future
But why?
We all bleed red
We all breathe air
We all have an ordinary human body
We live in a world where certain people are hated for the
colour they were born in,
The colour they can't change
A world where even children are humiliated because of their
skin colour
But why?
We all bleed red
We all breathe air
We all have an ordinary human body
Don't we all live in this world?

**Dunmininu Adesanya (12)**
Upton-By-Chester High School, Upton-By-Chester

# A Poem On Bullying

Bullies are cruel and unkind, though they take many forms.
From teasing words that cut like knives to physical force,
It's hard to stand up and be brave when it storms.
The taunts can seem never-ending, as if a constant source.
But all must stop, with strength and courage we will rise,
An end to this suffering, all of us must devise,
End the cycle of pain, lift us from the despair.
Let us stand together, no longer broken apart,
Bravely standing up for each other, heal our broken hearts.
Be strong and united, together we'll make a start.

**Joanne Pereira (13)**
Upton-By-Chester High School, Upton-By-Chester

# I Can See You

I can see you standing there looking at me,
your glowing eyes filled with pride,
I can see you waiting for me to walk through each open
door of opportunity,
overcoming each tide,

I can see you protecting me over each small hurdle,
I can see you shooting me at each and every shining star,

I can see you holding my hand when things get hard,
I can see you ready to catch me when I slip and fall,

Now I can't see you,
but I know you're still there,
I can't see you,
but I can feel your warm, curly hair.

## Etty Wren (12)
Upton-By-Chester High School, Upton-By-Chester

# Anger

I can feel it again
That flickery little fire inside of me.
My face slowly turning red
while I hold my breath
because I can't yell nor scream.
My knuckles turning white
from clenching my fist so tight.

A few tears begin to rise in my eyes.
Sometimes you can have so much anger
it can turn into teary moments.
You are unable to express your pain and how much anger it
causes you.
Soon that flickery little fire becomes a raging forest fire
that sadly utterly consumes you.

## Belle Flynn (14)
Upton-By-Chester High School, Upton-By-Chester

# Leaves

Yellow, orange and brown
cold, lonely, waiting to be found
the moonlight cascades down
onto the yellow, orange and brown
feeling lonely and down
but the leaves don't mind
they hide that frown,
and turn it upside down

Yellow, orange and brown
reserved, frigid, still waiting to be found
the clouds circle around
all around the yellow, orange and brown
finally, they have been found
and now they don't have to hide that frown
or turn it upside down.

**Ellie Dutton (12)**
Upton-By-Chester High School, Upton-By-Chester

# Will This Heartache Ever End?

I thought of you with love today
But that is nothing new
As it was our anniversary
January twenty-first like every other year
Except for this one without you, my dear.

I went and whined
Alas, what is the point of my life
Without the great love we shared
My vision impaired
As the tears I had shed drenched my bed.
Your death was like a light went out of my life
Shadows were everywhere
And daylight never came
Even if it did it would never be the same
Sleep my love
The peace belongs to you
Your life's work is done once and for all
Your place in my heart will always stay
And it has now turned black and grey
I can't count how many times I've cried
It is as if it was I who had died.
Will this heartache ever end?
How long will I have to wait until we meet in Heaven, my
ever long-lasting friend?

## Sihaam Ismail (14)
UTC Sheffield Olympic Legacy Park, Sheffield

# Perfect Women

They march down the street
Row by row,
Years of having men say *no!*

Pretty dresses,
Pretty heels,
Pretty face,
Perfect women? Are we?

No. It's the men.

Fancy suits,
Fancy hairdos,
Fancy jobs.

We bleed the same blood,
We speak the same sounds,
But somehow
We are different.

Perfect cook,
Perfect cleaner,
Perfect mum,
Perfect women? Are we?

No. It's the men.

Four walls,
One roof,
Something we call home,
Somehow it became our own prison.

Misery became our new happiness,
We scream,
We shout,
We cry,
You don't seem to see our pain.

Power,
Money
And ego blind you.

Perfect women? We want to be.

## Shayla Staniland (13) & Ava Cook (14)
UTC Sheffield Olympic Legacy Park, Sheffield

# Waterfall

What truly reflects that current
that we set on its trajectory,
gorges, rivers and valleys carving their way
in history and future bravery?

Each ebb and flow, each dip and crack
leaving and projecting its unique track,
on our achievements, our failures,
our futures.

Until it arrives at the waterfall.
The terminal point, the edge,
where lies meet truth, memories are forged and forgotten.
Our current and our journey come to a cascading close.

But what truly reflects the
current that we set on its trajectory?
Its course,
its conclusion.

**Jacob Johnston (14)**
UTC Sheffield Olympic Legacy Park, Sheffield

# Burnt Out

Not long ago, I walked on barbed wire.
It didn't matter; I was on fire.

The more I walked the further the end appeared.
It didn't matter; I was prepared.

Not long after I reached the end,
It didn't matter... there was
Another path of barbed wire.

I thought I was prepared for the sacrifices that would
Come with achieving my goal,
If only I didn't abandon the easier path,
I had multiple chances to turn back without consequence,
Now I am left with no sustenance to push me forward,
The source of my ignition is gone,
And I am burnt out.

## Khadija Sughra (13)
UTC Sheffield Olympic Legacy Park, Sheffield

# Self-Image

As I look in the mirror, I think to myself
*Why must I have this self-image of me?* I always see
People like me wanting to be free.
At first I didn't understand why life is like this.
However, I know acceptance is my only wish.

Lately, I've been ignoring the negative thoughts
And it's not easy.
Then again, no one ever said the journey would be breezy.
The journey might be hard, but I know life can go far.

**Jessica Harrison-Saunby (14)**
UTC Sheffield Olympic Legacy Park, Sheffield

# Lost Love

My eyes were filled with heavy love,
Her actions as elegant as a dove.
Some may say love at first sight,
But she makes my heart tight.

But on that dreadful day
My love eventually slipped away -
Tears prick at my soulful eyes,
My mind becoming my own demise.

A horrid pain in my chest consumes me
Removing all my thoughtful glee;
I attempt to catch my breath
Feeling as if I will be met with death.

I will forever remember my first love,
Like I said, she was as elegant as a dove.
Her heart filled with compassion and joy
And her bravery stronger than a mighty boy.

I ponder through all my thoughts,
Memories of her began to wash away.
As night turns into a pleasant day -
She begins to drift away.

**Summer Martin (12)**
Writhlington School, Writhlington

# Realisation

It's hard, you know,
trying to grieve
when the person is still alive.

All the thoughts of what I've seen and heard
yet he'll still be there.
That's the problem.

All the things he's said,
I'll never forget those horrific things,
yet, I know he'll be moving on
like I've forgiven and forgotten.

Sometimes I wish it never happened -
because I wouldn't be in this mess,
but then I remember that
whatever is thrown at you
will only make you stronger.

Although I know he's still my dad,
I don't think I care anymore,
sometimes I don't think I love him anymore.

There was a hole at first, in my heart.
But soon,
after everything,
it disappeared, like it never belonged there -
but I know that hole will never come back;

it's been filled
and there's no room for him anymore.

## Alice Derry (15)

Writhlington School, Writhlington

# Lemonade

You push a litre of lemonade down
The chute, fingertips tracing the
Bulging intruders
Blistering on your lemon.

The bathroom walls cave in
Like the swallowing throat of a cobra;
Your shameful throne greets you.

Take your rightful place. Shove
A spatula down your
Pitcher. Undress your shield of rinds.
Wring lemons into lemonade.

Your fingers grip the cold cliffs
Of the bowl like it's a steering wheel
Gyrating out of control.
Your curdled pulp sits staring back at you,
Singeing and numbing.

The sour, acrid aftertaste ploughs
Into the air. The only way out is further in.

Above purpling knees, you
Pray you'd live till the day
You are zested into
Bones wrapped only
In fracturing pith.

## Charmaine Chan (17)

Wycombe Abbey School, High Wycombe

# Young Writers Information

We hope you have enjoyed reading this book – and that you will continue to in the coming years.

If you're the parent or family member of an enthusiastic poet or story writer, do visit our website **www.youngwriters.co.uk/subscribe** and sign up to receive news, competitions, writing challenges and tips, activities and much, much more! There's lots to keep budding writers motivated!

If you would like to order further copies of this book, or any of our other titles, then please give us a call or order via your online account.

Young Writers
Remus House
Coltsfoot Drive
Peterborough
PE2 9BF
(01733) 890066
info@youngwriters.co.uk

Join in the conversation!
Tips, news, giveaways and much more!

 **YoungWritersUK**    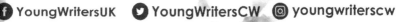 **YoungWritersCW**     **youngwriterscw**